COMMUNICATOR II

The Comprehensive Course in Functional English

Steven J. Molinsky
Bill Bliss

Contributing Authors
Susan Siegel
Carol Piñeiro

Prentice Hall Regents
Upper Saddle River, New Jersey 07458

Pelcastre A. R.

Library of Congress Cataloguing-in-Publication Data

Molinsky, Steven J.
    Communicator II : the comprehensive course in functional English /
Steven J. Molinsky, Bill Bliss ; contributing authors, Susan Siegel,
Carol Pinero ; [photographs, Paul Tañedo ; illustrations, Richard E.
Hill.
      p. cm.
    Includes index.
    ISBN 0-13-340688-1
    1. English language—Textbooks for foreign speakers.
2. Communication—Problems, exercises, etc.   I. Bliss, Bill.
II. Title.
PE1128.M6724   1995
428.2'4—dc20

94-23686
CIP

Publisher: Tina Carver
Director of Production and Manufacturing: David Riccardi
Editorial Production/Design Manager: Dominick Mosco
Production Supervision: Janet Johnston
Page Composition: Ken Liao
Production Coordinator: Ray Keating
Cover Coordinator: Merle Krumper

Cover Designer: Marianne Frasco
Cover Art: Todd Ware
Interior Design: Kenny Beck

Photographs: Paul Tañedo
Illustrations: Richard E. Hill

© 1995 by Prentice Hall Regents
Prentice-Hall, Inc.
A Simon & Schuster Company
Englewood Cliffs, New Jersey 07632

Printed in the United States of America

10   9   8   7   6   5   4   3

ISBN 0-13-340668-1

Prentice-Hall International (UK) Limited, London
Prentice-Hall of Australia Pty. Limited, Sydney
Prentice-Hall Canada Inc., Toronto
Prentice-Hall Hispanoamericana, S.A., Mexico
Prentice-Hall of India Private Limited, New Delhi
Prentice-Hall of Japan, Inc., Tokyo
Simon & Schuster Asia Pte. Ltd., Singapore
Editora Prentice-Hall do Brasil, Ltda., Rio de Janeiro

Contents

Communicator is a functional English course for adult and secondary school learners of English. It is intended for students who have been exposed to the essentials of intermediate-level grammar and who have already mastered the usage of English for everyday life situations. The text builds upon and reinforces this foundation and prepares students for higher-level language skills required for effective interpersonal communication. *Communicator* is organized functionally and incorporates integrated coverage of grammar and topics.

The Dimensions of Communication: Function, Form, and Content

Communicator provides dynamic, communicative practice that involves students in lively interactions based on the content of real-life contexts and situations. Every lesson offers students simultaneous practice with one or more functions, the grammatical forms needed to express those functions competently, and the contexts and situations in which the functions and grammar are used. This "tri-dimensional clustering" of function, form, and content is the organizing principle behind each lesson and the cornerstone of the *Communicator* approach to functional syllabus design. *Communicator* offers students broad exposure to uses of language in a variety of relevant contexts: in community, academic, employment, home, and social settings. The text gives students practice using a variety of registers; from the formal language someone might use in a job interview, with a customer, or when speaking to an authority figure; to the informal language someone would use when talking with family members, co-workers, or friends.

A special feature of the course is the treatment of discourse strategies — initiating conversations and topics, interrupting, hesitating, asking for clarification, and other conversation skills.

An Overview

Chapter-Opening Photos

Each chapter-opening page features two photographs of situations that depict key functions presented in the chapter. Students make predictions about who the people are and what they might be saying to each other. In this way, students have the opportunity to share what they already know and to relate the chapter's content to their own lives and experiences.

Guided Conversations

Guided conversations are the dialogs and exercises that are the central learning devices in *Communicator*. Each lesson begins with a model guided conversation that illustrates the use of one or more functions and the structures they require, all in the context of a meaningful exchange of communication. Key functional expressions in the models are in bold-face type and are footnoted, referring students to short lists of alternative expressions for accomplishing the functions. In the exercises that follow, students create new conversations by placing new content into the framework of the model, and by using any of the alternative functional expressions.

Original Student Conversations

Each lesson ends with an open-ended exercise that offers students the opportunity to create and present original conversations based on the functional theme of the lesson and the alternative expressions. Students contribute content based on their experiences, ideas, and imaginations. The ultimate objective of each lesson is to enable students to use functional expressions competently in creating their own original conversations.

Check-Up

This section features a variety of follow-up exercises and activities:

- **Function Check** exercises provide review and reinforcement of functional expressions presented in the chapter.
- **Grammar Check** exercises offer practice with key grammar structures featured in the guided conversation lessons.
- **Listening Exercises** give students intensive listening practice that focuses on functional communication.
- **InterChange** activities provide opportunities for students to relate lesson content to their own lives.
- **InterCultural Connections** activities offer rich opportunities for cross-cultural comparison.
- **In Your Own Words** activities provide opportunities for writing and discussion of important issues presented in the chapter.
- **InterView** activities encourage students to interview each other as well as people in the community.
- **InterAct!** activities provide opportunities for role playing and cooperative learning.
- **Reading** passages in every chapter are designed to provide interesting and stimulating content for class discussion. These selections are also available on the accompanying audiotapes for additional listening comprehension practice.

Communicators

This end-of-chapter activity offers students the opportunity to create and to present "guided role plays." Each activity consists of a model that students can practice and then use as a basis for their original presentations. Students should be encouraged to be inventive and to use new vocabulary in these presentations and should feel free to adapt and expand the model any way they wish.

Scenes & Improvisations

These "free role plays" appear after every third chapter, offering review and synthesis of functions and conversation strategies in the three preceding chapters. Students are presented with eight scenes depicting conversations between people in various situations. The students determine who the people are and what they are talking about, and then improvise based on their perceptions of the scenes' characters, contexts, and situations. These improvisations promote students' absorption of the preceding chapters' functions and strategies into their repertoire of active language use.

Support and Reference Sections

- **End-of-Chapter Summaries** provide complete lists of functional expressions in each chapter.
- A **Notes and Commentary** section in the Appendix provides notes on language usage, grammar, and culture; commentaries on the characters, contexts, and situations; and explanations of idiomatic and colloquial expressions.
- An **Inventory of Functions and Conversation Strategies** in the Appendix offers a comprehensive display of all functional expressions in the text.

- An **Index** provides a convenient reference for locating functions and grammar in the text.

Suggested Teaching Strategies

We encourage you, in using *Communicator*, to develop approaches and strategies that are compatible with your own teaching style and the needs and abilities of your students. While the program does not require any specific method or technique in order to be used effectively, you may find it helpful to review and try out some of the following suggestions. (Specific step-by-step instructions may be found in the *Communicator Teacher's Guide*.)

Chapter-Opening Photos

Have students talk about the people and the situations and, as a class or in pairs, predict what the characters might be saying to each other. Students in pairs or small groups may enjoy practicing role plays based on these scenes and then presenting them to the class.

Guided Conversations

1. LISTENING: With books closed, have students listen to the model conversation — presented by you, by a pair of students, or on the audiotape.
2. DISCUSSION: Have students discuss the model conversation: Who are the people? What is the situation?
   At this point, you should call students' attention to any related Language and Culture Notes, which can be found in the Appendix.
3. READING: Have students follow along as two students present the model with books open.
4. PRACTICE: Have students practice the model conversation in pairs, small groups, or as a class.
5. ALTERNATIVE EXPRESSIONS: Present to the class each sentence of the dialog containing a footnoted expression. Call on different students to present the same sentence, replacing the footnoted expression with its alternatives. (You can cue students to do this quickly by asking, "What's another way of saying that?" or "How else could he/she/you say that?")
6. PAIR PRACTICE (optional): Have pairs of students simultaneously practice all the exercises, using the footnoted expressions or any of their alternatives.
7. PRESENTATION: Call on pairs of students to present the exercises, using the footnoted expressions or any of their alternatives. Before students present, set the scene by describing the characters and the context, or have students do this themselves.

Original Student Conversations

In these activities, which follow the guided conversations at the end of each lesson, have pairs of students create and present original conversations based on the theme of the lesson and any of the alternative expressions. Encourage students to be inventive as they create their characters and situations. (You may want students to prepare their original conversations as homework, then practice them the next day with another student and present them to the class. In that way, students can review the previous day's lesson without actually having to repeat the specific exercises already covered.)

InterChange

Have students first work in pairs and then share with the class what they talked about.

In Your Own Words

This activity is designed for both writing practice and discussion. Have students discuss the activity as a class, in pairs, or in small groups. Then have students write their responses at home, share their written work with other students, and discuss in class. Students may enjoy keeping a journal of their written work. If time permits, you may want to write a response in each student's journal, sharing your own opinions and experiences as well as reacting to what the student has written. If you are keeping portfolios of students' work, these compositions serve as excellent examples of students' progress in learning English.

InterCultural Connections

Have students do the activity as a class, in pairs, or in small groups.

InterView

Have students circulate around the room to conduct their interviews, or have students interview people outside the class. Students should then report back to the class about their interviews.

InterAct!

Have pairs of students practice role-playing the activity and then present their role plays to the class.

Reading

Have students discuss the topic of the reading beforehand, using the pre-reading questions suggested in the *Teacher's Guide*. Have students then read the passage silently, or have them listen to the passage and take notes as you read it or play the audiotape. The *Teacher's Guide* also contains a list of questions designed to check students' comprehension of the passage.

Communicators

Have students practice the model, using the same steps listed above for guided conversations. Then have pairs of students create and present original conversations, using the model dialog as a guide. Encourage students to be inventive and to use new vocabulary. (You may want to assign this exercise as homework, having students prepare their conversations, practice them the next day with another student, and then present them to the class.) Students should present their conversations without referring to the written text, but they should also not memorize them. Rather, they should feel free to adapt and expand them any way they wish.

Scenes & Improvisations

Have students talk about the people and the situations, and then present role plays based on the scenes. Students may refer back to previous lessons as a resource, but they should not simply re-use specific conversations. (You may want to assign these exercises as written homework, having students prepare their conversations, practice them the next day with another student, and then present them to the class.)

In conclusion, we have attempted to offer students a communicative, meaningful, and lively way of practicing the functions of English, along with the grammar structures needed to express them competently. While conveying to you the substance of our textbook, we hope that we have also conveyed the spirit: that learning to communicate in English can be genuinely interactive . . . truly relevant to our students' lives . . . and fun!

Steven J. Molinsky
Bill Bliss

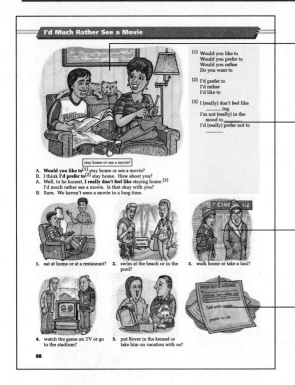

A **model conversation** offers initial practice with the functions and structures of the lesson.

Key functional expressions are in bold-face type and are footnoted, referring students to a box containing alternative expressions for accomplishing the functions.

In the **exercises**, students create conversations by placing new contexts, content, or characters into the model, and by using any of the alternative functional expressions.

The **open-ended exercise** at the end of each lesson asks students to create and present original conversations on the theme of the lesson and any of the alternative expressions.

For example:

Exercise 1 might be completed by placing the new exercise content into the existing model:

A. Would you like to eat at home or at a restaurant?
B. I think I'd prefer to eat at home. How about you?
A. Well, to be honest, I really don't feel like eating at home. I'd much rather eat at a restaurant. Is that okay with you?
B. Sure. We haven't eaten at a restaurant in a long time.

Exercise 2 might be completed by using the new exercise content *and* some of the alternative functional expressions:

A. Would you prefer to swim at the beach or in the pool?
B. I think I'd like to swim at the beach. How about you?
A. Well, to be honest, I'm not really in the mood to swim at the beach. I'd much rather swim in the pool. Is that okay with you?
B. Sure. We haven't swum in the pool in a long time.

Using the Footnotes

1. ( ) indicates that the word or words are optional. For example, the sentence:

   I'm (very) sorry to hear that. = I'm sorry to hear that.
                                                   I'm very sorry to hear that.

2. / indicates that the words on either side of the / mark are interchangeable. For example, the sentence:

   I don't/can't believe it! = I don't believe it!
                                          I can't believe it!

3. Sometimes the ( ) and / symbols appear together. For example, the sentence:

   I'm not (completely/absolutely) positive. = I'm not positive.
                                                        I'm not completely positive.
                                                        I'm not absolutely positive.

4. Sometimes the footnote indicates that an alternative expression requires a change in the grammar of the sentence. For example, the sentences:

   I don't feel like _____ing. = I don't feel like dancing.
   I'd prefer not to _____. = I'd prefer not to dance.

1

INVITATIONS
OBLIGATIONS
LEAVE TAKING

One of these high school students is inviting the other to do something this weekend. Which person do you think is making the invitation? What do you think they're saying to each other?

Susan and Patricia bumped into each other on the street a short time ago, and they've been talking for a while. Now they're finishing their conversation. What do you think they're saying to each other?

go to the zoo

(1) Would you like to _____?
How would you like to _____?
Do you want to _____?
Would you be interested in _____ing?
Let's _____.

(2) I'd love to.
I'd like to.
I'd like that.
That sounds like fun.
That sounds great/ terrific/wonderful.
That would be great/ terrific/wonderful.
I'd be happy to/glad to.

[stronger]
I'd be delighted to/ thrilled to.

A. **Would you like to**(1) go to the zoo this Sunday?
B. **I'd love to.**(2) I haven't gone to the zoo in a long time.
A. Me neither. That's why I thought going to the zoo might be a nice idea.

1. see a ballgame

2. play basketball

3. go sailing

4. take a ride in the country

5. pick strawberries

Invite somebody to do something.

2

Listening: *What's the Meaning?*

Listen and choose the answer that is closest in meaning to the sentence you have heard.

1. a. Howard likes tonight's theater.
   b. How would you like to meet her tonight?
   c. Do you want to go to the theater this evening?

2. a. I thought about going canoeing this afternoon.
   b. Would you like to go canoeing this afternoon?
   c. Who's going canoeing this afternoon?

3. a. The sound is terrific.
   b. Pat had a terrific idea.
   c. That would be great.

4. a. It's been a while since I've gone to a hockey game.
   b. I haven't played hockey in a long time.
   c. I haven't played soccer in a while.

5. a. You're crazy to travel around the world.
   b. I'd love to travel around the world.
   c. Do you want to travel around the world?

6. a. Those gold necklaces are interesting.
   b. How would you like to purchase some gold necklaces?
   c. Would you try to buy me some gold necklaces?

7. a. I'll show you the lighted room.
   b. You'll be happy to know your room is well lighted.
   c. I'd be happy to take you to your room.

8. a. We're going to spend this Sunday at the beach.
   b. I spent a lot of money the other day at the beach.
   c. I like the idea of spending the day in the sun at the beach.

9. a. There's going to be a concert in the park on Sunday.
   b. Would you be interested in going to a concert with me?
   c. I'm going to a concert this Sunday with Mark.

Grammar Check: *Gerunds and Infinitives*

1. How about (to go (going)) for a walk?
2. Do you want ((to see) seeing) a play tonight?
3. I'd like ((to have) having) a little party this Friday night.
4. I thought (to eat (eating)) at Antonio's would be a good idea.
5. I'm tired of working. What about (to go (going)) out for ice cream?
6. Would you be interested in (to buy (buying)) some Girl Scout cookies?

Playing tennis.

Going to the beach.

Going for a long bike ride.

Take a survey of students in your class and five other people you know. Ask what everybody's favorite weekend activity is.

Tabulate the results and compare with other students' surveys. Then extend an invitation to people you interviewed to join you in YOUR favorite weekend activity!

see a movie?

study for my college entrance exams

(1) If you're not busy,
    If you're free,
    If you don't have any
       other plans,

(2) Would you (by any
       chance) be interested in
       _____ing?
    You wouldn't (by any
       chance) be interested in
       _____ing, would you?

(3) can't
    won't be able to

(4) I have to
    I've got to
    I'm supposed to

(5) asking
    inviting me
    the invitation

A. **If you're not busy,**(1) **would you by any chance be interested in**(2) seeing a movie with me this Saturday?
B. I'd love to, but I **can't.**(3) **I have to**(4) study for my college entrance exams.
A. That's too bad.
B. Thanks for **asking,**(5) though. Maybe we can see a movie some other time.

go out for dinner?

1. attend my cousin's wedding

have a picnic?

2. help my parents with the "spring cleaning"

see a play?

3. take care of my little sister

go dancing?

4. participate in our annual school concert

play miniature golf?

5. work on my science project

Invite somebody to do something.

Function Check: *What's My Line?*

Choose the appropriate line for Speaker B.

A   **B**

1. If you're not busy, would you be interested in seeing a play this Friday night?
   - a. Thanks for telling me.
   - b. I have to.
   - c. I'd love to, but I can't. *(circled)*

2. Rick, you wouldn't by any chance be interested in helping me work on my car, would you?
   - a. I've got to.
   - b. I'd be happy to.
   - c. Thanks for asking.

3. I'm sorry you won't be able to join me at the ballet.
   - a. I'd be delighted to.
   - b. Me too, but thanks for the invitation.
   - c. I'm not busy.

4. How would you like to go deep-sea fishing with me, Carol?
   - a. I'm supposed to go fishing.
   - b. If you don't have any other plans.
   - c. That sounds like fun.

5. Let's visit the museum this afternoon!
   - a. I'd like to, but I can't. I have to do my homework.
   - b. Thanks for asking, though.
   - c. That's nice.

6. It's too bad you can't go hiking with me.
   - a. That sounds like fun.
   - b. Maybe we can go hiking, though.
   - c. Thanks for inviting me, though.

InterChange

Things to Do!

We all have things to do—errands, work and school responsibilities, and family obligations. Talk with a partner about things YOU have to do.

> *I have to . . .*   *I've got to . . .*   *I'm supposed to . . .*

Tell the class what you have to do, and decide who the *busiest* person in the class is. If you wish, invite each other to do things. Some classmates will be free, and others won't be because they have *things to do*!

I'm organizing a company picnic for this Saturday.

work overtime

(1) Can you come?
Do you think you can come?
Do you think you'd be able to come?
Would you be able to come?
Can you make it?
Do you think you can make it?

(2) Let me check and get back to you.
I'll check and let you know.

(3) I'll do my best.
I'll try as hard as I can.

A. I'm organizing a company picnic for this Saturday. **Can you come?**(1)
B. I'd love to, but I'm not sure I can. I think I'm supposed to work overtime.
A. That's too bad. Is there any chance you could possibly get out of working overtime?
B. I'm not sure. **Let me check and get back to you.**(2)
A. Okay, but please try to come. It won't be much of a company picnic without you!
B. It's nice of you to say that. **I'll do my best.**(3)

I'm having a slumber party this Saturday night.

1. baby-sit

I'm planning a family reunion for next April 20th.

2. speak at my firm's annual meeting

I'm throwing a surprise party for my husband's birthday this Friday night.

3. be on duty

I'm putting together a softball game for this coming Saturday afternoon.

4. help my landlord paint the hallway

I'm scheduling a "pot luck supper" for the first Sunday in June.

5. collect for the Heart Fund

Invite somebody to a special event you're planning.

6

Listening: *Who's Talking?*

Listen and decide what the relationship between the two speakers is.

1. a. employee–employee
   b. mother–child
   c. teacher–student

2. a. groom–bride
   b. friend–friend
   c. brother–sister

3. a. grandfather–grandmother
   b. father–son
   c. grandfather–grandfather

4. a. cook–cook
   b. baseball player– baseball player
   c. barber–customer

5. a. government official– government official
   b. teenager–teenager
   c. mother–father

6. a. teammate–teammate
   b. sailor–sailor
   c. prisoner–guard

7. a. soldier–soldier
   b. TV producer– TV producer
   c. client–client

8. a. plant store owner– customer
   b. patient–patient
   c. doctor–doctor

9. a. tennis player– tennis player
   b. tenant–tenant
   c. boss–employee

gard

Grammar Check: *Modals*

1. I've got theater tickets for this Saturday. ((Can) Should   Might) you come with me?

2. I'd like to, but I'm not sure I (would   can't   can).

3. Is there any chance you (should   could   have to) possibly get out of babysitting tonight?

4. Do you think you (can   would   could) be able to come to the tennis match with me?

5. Thanks for asking, but I (have to   would   shouldn't) finish my science project.

6. Do you think your parents (would   should   can) make it to cousin Sally's wedding?

7.

> *Boy! Tickets to a rock concert! I'd love to go, but I (can   could   can't).*

InterCultural Connections

Match

_c_ 1. a company picnic	**a.**	a party for someone who doesn't know about it
_d_ 2. a slumber party	**b.**	a get-together of all the relatives
_b_ 3. a family reunion	**c.**	a get-together of all the employees
_a_ 4. a surprise party	**d.**	a group of children who sleep overnight at one of their houses
_e_ 5. a pot-luck supper	**e.**	a meal where everyone brings a different dish

Are these events common in your country? Do you think these are worthwhile events? Why or why not? What kinds of parties and get-togethers are popular in your country? What do people do at these events?

dinner
this Saturday evening
7:00

you and your wife

(1) We'd like to invite you and
your *wife* over
We'd like to have you and
your *wife* over
We'd like you and your *wife*
to be our guests
We'd like you and your *wife*
to join us

(2) Thank you/Thanks for the
invitation.
Thank you/Thanks for
inviting us.
I appreciate the invitation.
It's (very) nice of you to
invite us.

(3) very happy
very glad
pleased
delighted

(4) How does *7:00* sound?
Is *7:00* convenient/all right?
Would *7:00* be convenient/
all right?

A. **We'd like to invite you and your wife over**[1] for dinner this
Saturday evening. Would you be able to come?
B. This Saturday evening?
A. Yes. We hope you'll be able to join us.
B. **Thank you for the invitation.**[2] We'd be **very happy**[3] to
come.
A. Good.
B. What time should we plan to arrive?
A. **How does 7:00 sound?**[4]
B. 7:00? That's fine. We'll be looking forward to it.

brunch
this Sunday
noon

1. you and your husband

a barbecue
this Saturday
afternoon
2:00

2. you and your family

dinner
this Friday
evening
6:00

3. you and your wife

a party celebrating our 15th
wedding anniversary
this Saturday evening
7:30

4. you and your fiancé

a small get-together we're
having
this Saturday evening
8:00

5. you and your fiancée

Invite somebody to
bring along a family
member to an event
at your home.

Function Check: *What's the Expression?*

1. A. We'd like _____ you and Jeff
        over to play bridge this
        Friday night.
        a. to invite
        b. to join
        c. to come
    B. This Friday night?

2. A. Yes. Would you _____?
        a. be able to come
        b. invite you and your
            husband over
        c. be happy to come

3. B. Thank you _____.
        a. for inviting
        b. for the convenience
        c. for the invitation

4.   We'd be _____ to come over.
        a. please
        b. delighted
        c. thrill
        What time should we plan
        to arrive?

5. A. Would 7:30 _____?
        a. sound convenient
        b. look forward to it
        c. be all right
    B. That's fine. See you then.

InterAct!

Problem Situation

Your boss is inviting you to dinner this Saturday, but you're busy.

A. We'd like you and your wife to join us for dinner this
    Friday evening.
B. Oh, I'm sorry. We're going to a movie with some friends.
A. How about NEXT Friday?
B. Next Friday? I'm not sure. I think we might be busy. I'll
    have to let you know. Thank you for inviting us, though.

Do you think this employee acted appropriately? Talk it
over with a partner. If you feel he acted inappropriately,
rewrite the conversation between the employee and the
boss and present it to the class.

have this car back at the rental agency by 2:00

(1) bumped into
    ran into

(2) be going
    get going
    be on my way
    be getting on my way

(3) I need to
    I have to
    I've got to
    I'm supposed to

(4) get together soon
    keep in touch
    stay in touch

(5) Take care.
    Take it easy.

(6) So long.
    Good-bye.
    Bye.
    Bye-bye.
    See you.

A. Well, it's been really nice seeing you again.
B. Yes, it has. I'm glad we **bumped into**(1) each other.
A. Me, too. You know, I think I should **be going**(2) now. **I need to**(3) have this car back at the rental agency by 2:00.
B. Actually, I should get going, too.
A. Let's **get together soon.**(4)
B. Okay. I'll call you.
A. **Take care.**(5)
B. **So long.**(6)

1. get these packages to the post office before it closes

2. finish my lunch hour a little early today

3. pick up a few things at the supermarket on my way home

4. be at my piano lesson by 4:00

5. reach Denver by 7:00 tonight

It's time to say good-bye to a friend you've just bumped into.

Listening: *Conclusions*

Listen and choose the best conclusion.

1. a. They've just met.
    b. They've known each other for a long time.
    c. They're talking on the telephone.

2. a. This is the end of the conversation.
    b. This conversation took place at 11:30.
    c. They're talking about a past event.

3. a. Sally and Tom are married.
    b. Sally and Tom are talking about going out on a date.
    c. Sally is not free Saturday night.

4. a. Louise and Carol are happy to see each other again.
    b. Louise has to rush off.
    c. Louise has to pick up her son.

5. a. Larry and Eddie have been studying for an exam together.
    b. Larry and Eddie have just begun their conversation.
    c. Larry and Eddie both have to leave.

6. a. Susan and her brother accepted the invitation.
    b. Susan and her brother live with their grandparents.
    c. Susan and her brother already have plans for Thanksgiving.

7. a. This is the beginning of their conversation.
    b. This is the end of their conversation.
    c. Both speakers live in town.

InterCultural Connections

The "Ritual" of Saying Good-bye

All the people on page 10 have been talking for some time and are ready to end their conversations. But they don't just say "good-bye!" They go through what is a typical polite ritual in the United States.

They express pleasure at having seen one another.

It's been really nice seeing you again.

I'm glad we bumped into each other.

Both speakers say they need to leave.

I think I should be going now.

I should get going, too.

Reasons for leaving are given.

I need to have this car back at the rental agency by 2:00.

They promise to see one another again.

Let's get together soon.

Okay. I'll call you.

They finally say their actual "good-byes."

See you soon.

So long.

Why do you think these people take such a long time to say good-bye? How would people in YOUR country end this conversation? With a partner, re-enact the scene from your country's perspective.

get to my English class

A **By the way,**(1) **what time is it?**(2)
B. It's about 1:30.
A. 1:30?! Already?! I didn't realize it was so late.
B. I didn't either.
A. **I've really got to go now.**(3) **I've got to**(4) get to my English class.
B. You'd better hurry! **See you soon.**(5)
A. So long.
B. Bye.

(1) By the way,
    Incidentally,

(2) What time is it?
    What time do you have?
    Do you have the time?

(3) I've (really) got to go now.
    I've (really) got to be
        going now.
    I (really) have to go now.
    I'd (really) better go now.
    I (really) need to go now.
    I (really) should go now.
    I have to/I've got to run.
    I have to/I've got to
        get going.

(4) I've got to
    I have to
    I need to

(5) (I'll) see you soon/later/
        tomorrow/next week/ . . .

1. get to the bank before
   it closes

2. pick up my daughter at
   school

3. catch a 3:00 plane

4. be home in time for dinner

5. put my makeup on before
   the show begins

It's late! You'd better hurry! Say good-bye to a friend you've been talking with.

Function Check: *What's the Expression?*

1. _____, what time is it?
   a. By way
   b. Incidentally
   c. Take care

2. I've _____ go now.
   a. really got to
   b. better
   c. have to

3. Do you _____?
   a. get the time
   b. better go now
   c. have the time

4. I didn't _____ it was so late.
   a. really
   b. either
   c. realize

5. _____ tomorrow.
   a. I'll see you soon
   b. Good-bye
   c. I'll see you

6. I'd _____ go now.
   a. better
   b. should
   c. have to

7. Let's _____ soon.
   a. be getting on my way
   b. get together
   c. keep in touch

8. I've got to _____.
   a. good-bye
   b. take care
   c. get going

9. It's nearly 6:00 P.M. _____
   a. What time is it?
   b. Take it easy.
   c. I should run.

10. _____ be at the hospital by 5:30 A.M.! I'm late.
    a. I'm supposed to
    b. I get to
    c. I'll need to

11. Well, I didn't realize it was so late. _____.
    a. I'll see you soon.
    b. Let's keep in touch soon.
    c. I really should.

12. Let's stay _____.
    a. on my way
    b. before it closes
    c. in touch

13. *It's midnight! I've got to go. _____.*
    a. *See you.*
    b. *Too long.*
    c. *Be on my way.*

14. *It's late! _____.*
    a. *I'd better be on your way.*
    b. *You'd better hurry.*
    c. *See me soon.*

InterAct!

What if the conversations on page 12 had ended differently? Suppose the second speaker wanted to continue the conversation. For example:

Don't leave yet! You've got plenty of time!

Take your time! You won't be late!

Don't worry! There's lots of time!

With a partner, create new endings for the conversations and present them to the class.

Two friends are having trouble deciding when they can get together again. Practice this scene with a partner.

A. I'd love to continue this conversation, but I really need to go now. I have to get back to the office.

B. Well, let's get together soon.

A. Okay. Would you like to have lunch some day next week?

B. Sure. How about Monday?

A. Hmm. I'm afraid I can't make it on Monday. I've got to fly to Chicago on business.

B. Well, unfortunately I'm tied up on Tuesday. I'm supposed to have lunch with an important visitor from out of town, and I don't think there's any way I can get out of it. Are you free on Wednesday?

A. Wednesday? Let's see. Hmm. Somehow I think I've already got something scheduled for Wednesday. Oh, yes! I've got an appointment with my dentist to have my teeth cleaned, and it's essential that I keep it.

B. Well, I'm afraid Thursday is out for me. I'm expected to attend a meeting of our personnel committee, and it's very important for me to be there.

A. So that leaves Friday. I don't have any obligations or commitments on Friday. How about you?

B. Friday sounds good. Where should we meet?

A. You know, I really must be going now or I'll be very late. Can you give me a call tomorrow and we'll decide?

B. Fine. Speak to you then.

A. Sorry I have to rush off like this.

B. That's okay. I understand.

A. Good-bye.

B. So long. *Personal*

14

A. I'd love to continue this conversation, but I really need to go now. I have to _get back to my dorm_.

B. Well, let's get together soon.

A. Okay. Would you like to have lunch some day next week?

B. Sure. How about Monday?

A. Hmm. I'm afraid I can't make it on Monday. I've got to _cook to my friend house_.

B. Well, unfortunately I'm tied up on Tuesday. I'm supposed to _have dinner with an old friend_, and I don't think there's any way I can get out of it. Are you free on Wednesday?

A. Wednesday? Let's see. Hmm. Somehow I think I've already got something scheduled for Wednesday. Oh, yes! I've got an appointment with my _classmate to_ to _have studied, studied hard_, and it's essential that I keep it.

B. Well, I'm afraid Thursday is out for me. I'm expected to attend a _meeting of our personnel_, and it's very important for me to be there.

A. So that leaves Friday. I don't have any obligations or commitments on Friday. How about you?

B. Friday sounds good. Where should we meet?

A. You know, I really must be going now or I'll be very late. Can you give me a call tomorrow and we'll decide?

B. Fine. Speak to you then.

A. Sorry I have to rush off like this.

Now create an original scene with your partner. You're friends who can't decide which day to get together next week. You can use the model above as a guide, but feel free to adapt and expand it any way you wish.

Listening: *What's the Meaning?*

Listen and choose the answer that is closest in meaning to the sentence you have heard.

1. a. I'm scared to get off the phone now.
    b. I'm sorry, but I have to get off the plane now.
    c. I'm sorry, but I have to hang up now.

2. a. When did you get back to work?
    b. When do you have to finish working?
    c. When do you have to return to your office?

3. a. Let's have a party soon.
    b. Let's plan to see each other again soon.
    c. Let's write to each other soon.

4. a. I may wear a tie this morning.
    b. It's noon. I'll be right up.
    c. I might be busy all morning.

5. a. Meet me at 1:00 when you get out of work.
    b. I have a meeting at 1:00 that I have to go to.
    c. I'll really try to get out today at 1:00 after my meeting.

6. a. I'm sorry. I have to send this right away.
    b. Sorry I had to brush you off.
    c. Sorry I have to leave quickly.

Grammar Check: *Tense Review*

1.

Well, _____ really nice seeing you again.
   a. it has
   b. it's been
   c. it's being

2. I'm glad we _____ each other every few weeks.
    a. ran into
    b. run into
    c. have run into

3. You know, I _____ I should be going now.
    a. have thought
    b. had though
    c. think

4. I _____ be leaving, too. I have to pick up my wife at the station in ten minutes.
    a. supposed to
    b. have to
    c. am needing to

5. Let's get together soon. _____ you next week.
    a. I will have called
    b. I'll call
    c. I call

6. I _____ forward to seeing you and your family again soon.
    a. am looking
    b. looked
    c. have looked

7. Frank _____ get going now. He has a meeting at 10:00.
    a. had to
    b. has to
    c. has had to

8. All right. _____ in touch.
    a. Let's
    b. Will keep
    c. We'll keep

9. _____ to call you, but I haven't had a chance.
    a. I mean
    b. I've been meaning
    c. I try

Each society has its own notion of time that determines its social customs about punctuality. In some cultures, being early or on time for appointments is expected. If one comes late, it is considered disrespectful and a personal affront to the person waiting. In other cultures, being late is accepted and even expected because there are many reasons and circumstances that could cause a person not to be on time.

In the United States, people are usually expected to be on time for appointments or meetings. Fifteen minutes before or after the appointed hour is regarded as the borderline of acceptability for formal social gatherings, although there is more leeway at informal occasions.

Time is of the essence, however, at the workplace. In many large companies, workers have time cards that they must insert into time clocks. The clocks punch arrival and departure times on employees' time cards so that wages can be calculated and employee punctuality can be monitored. Many other places of employment use time sheets, on which employees are required to sign in and out at the beginning and end of a shift or a day's work.

Time-management experts are sometimes hired as consultants to give workshops to company staff on how to set priorities and accomplish tasks without wasting time. An innovation called flex-time has also been introduced to increase efficiency. Employees still put in a forty-hour work week, but they are free to arrive and leave between certain hours so as to beat the rush-hour traffic and better accommodate their work schedules to their home lives.

In many employment sectors where quick and efficient performance is of the utmost importance, employees are monitored by computers. Telephone operators, for example, must assist a certain number of customers per minute. If the computerized record of their productivity shows below-average performance, they are given a pep talk or a warning by their supervisors and are advised that they must conform to the company's standards.

The emphasis placed on time in American society can be summed up in the old adage "Time is money." In some cases, just a few minutes may be worth millions of dollars!

Time = Money

Group Simulation

You and a group of company executives are concerned about the efficiency of your company and are deciding what things you can do to improve the situation. Brainstorm ideas and make a presentation to the rest of the students in your class, who are your *board of directors*.

For Writing and Discussion

Time is money! *Time is of the essence!*

Do you agree with this? How important to you is the notion of time?

Here are the expressions you practiced in Chapter 1. Try to use as many as you can to expand your vocabulary and to add variety to your use of English.

Invitations

Extending . . .

Would you like to _____?
How would you like to _____?
Do you want to _____?
Would you be interested in _____ing?
How about _____ing?
Let's _____.

Would you (by any chance) be interested in _____ing?
You wouldn't (by any chance) be interested in _____ing, would you?

We'd like to invite you (and _____) ·over for _____.
We'd like to have you (and _____) over for _____.
We'd like you (and _____) to be our guest(s) for _____.
We'd like you (and _____) to join us for _____.

Can you come?
Do you think you can come?
Do you think you'd be able to come?
Would you be able to come?
Can you make it?
Do you think you can make it?

Please try to come.
We hope you'll be able to join us.

If you're not busy, . . .
If you're free, . . .
If you don't have any other plans, . . .

Accepting

I'd love to.
I'd like to.
I'd like that.
That sounds like fun.
That sounds great/terrific/wonderful.
That would be great/terrific/wonderful.
I'd be happy to/glad to.

[stronger]
I'd be delighted to/thrilled to.

We'd be $\left\{ \begin{array}{l} \text{very happy} \\ \text{very glad} \\ \text{pleased} \\ \text{delighted} \end{array} \right\}$ to come.

We'll be looking forward to it.

Thanks/Thank you for $\left\{ \begin{array}{l} \text{asking.} \\ \text{inviting me.} \\ \text{the invitation.} \end{array} \right\}$

I appreciate the invitation.
It's (very) nice of you to invite me.

Declining . . .

I'd love to, but I can't.
I'd love to, but I won't be able to.

Obligation

Expressing . . .

I have to _____.
I've got to _____.
I'm supposed to _____.
I need to _____.

I'm expected to _____.

I don't think there's any way I can get out of it.

I'm tied up on _____.
I've got something scheduled for _____.

I don't have any obligations or commitments on _____.

Ability/Inability

Inquiring about . . .

Can you _____?
Is there any chance you could (possibly) _____?
Would you be able to _____?

Expressing Inability

I can't.
I won't be able to.

I'm not sure I can.

I can't make it on _____.
I'm tied up on _____.

Leave Taking

(You know,) I think I should $\left\{ \begin{array}{l} \text{be going} \\ \text{get going} \\ \text{be on my way} \\ \text{be getting on my way} \end{array} \right\}$ (now).

(You know), I (really) must be going.
I've (really) got to go now.
I've (really) got to be going now.

I (really) have to go now.
I'd (really) better go now.
I (really) need to go now.
I (really) should go now.
I have to/I've got to run.
I have to/I've got to get going.

I should get going, too.

Well, it's been really nice seeing you again.

I'd love to continue this conversation but . . .

Let's get together soon.
Let's keep in touch.
Let's stay in touch.

(I'll) see you soon/later/tomorrow/ next week/ . . .

I'll call you.

Speak to you then.

Take care.
Take it easy.
So long.
Good-bye.
Bye.
Bye-bye.
See you.

Sorry I have to rush off like this.

Checking and Indicating Understanding

Checking One's Own Understanding

This Saturday evening?
7:00?

Directing/Redirecting a Conversation

By the way,
Incidentally,

2

ABILITY AND INABILITY
OBLIGATIONS

Rosa Benitez is interviewing Anthony Riccardi for a job.
She's asking him about his experience, skills, and
qualifications. What do you think they're saying to each
other?

Diane wasn't able to get an ingredient that Roy needs for
his recipe. What do you think they're saying to each other?

take shorthand
stenographer

(1) Can you
    Are you able to
    Do you know how to

(2) I've had a lot of
        experience
    I'm very good at

(3) consider yourself
    say you're

(4) experienced
    capable

(5) I would say so.
    Yes, I would.

A. **Can you**[1] take shorthand?
B. Yes, I can. **I've had a lot of experience**[2] taking shorthand.
A. Then you'd **consider yourself**[3] an **experienced**[4] stenographer?
B. **I would say so.**[5]

1. type technical reports
   typist

2. repair foreign cars
   mechanic

3. operate a computer
   data processor

4. fix window frames and doors
   carpenter

5. perform this operation
   surgeon

You're at a job interview. Tell how experienced you are.

alter men's clothing

(1) a lot of
a good deal of
a great deal of
years of

(2) I'm sure
I'm confident
I'm certain
I know

(3) I'd be able to
I could

(4) key
essential
major
significant

A. Can you alter men's clothing?
B. No, I can't. I've had **a lot of** (1) experience altering clothing, but I haven't altered MEN's clothing before. However, **I'm sure**(2) **I'd be able to**(3) learn quickly.
A. That would be important. Altering men's clothing is a **key**(4) part of the job.
B. Well, **I'm confident**(2) I can do it.

1. edit scientific manuscripts

2. design apartment buildings

3. operate a 70-millimeter projector

4. use a computerized cash register

5. drive a tractor-trailer truck

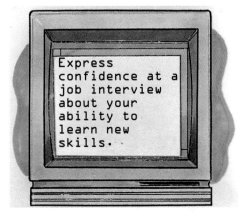

Express confidence at a job interview about your ability to learn new skills.

Vocabulary Check: *The Right Person*

1. A person who types technical reports is called a _____.
   a. typesetter
   b. typer
   c. typist ⓒ

2. A _____ is a person who takes shorthand.
   a. stenographer
   b. shorthander
   c. notetaker

3. A person who types information into a computer is _____.
   a. an operator
   b. a computer
   c. a data processor

4. A person who performs operations on patients is called _____.
   a. an operations manager
   b. a surgeon
   c. an operator

5. A _____ repairs cars.
   a. carpenter
   b. repairer
   c. mechanic

6. A person who makes furniture and works with wood is a _____.
   a. carpenter
   b. worker
   c. builder

7. A person who draws plans for buildings is _____.
   a. a drawer
   b. an architect
   c. a planner

8. A person who sews clothes is a _____.
   a. sewer
   b. machinist
   c. seamstress

Listening: *Conclusions*

Listen and choose the best conclusion.

1. a. Rich drives a stick-shift.
   b. Rich has never driven a stick-shift before. ⓑ
   c. Rich has never driven an automatic before.

2. a. Jerry has never used a computer before.
   b. Jerry's computer doesn't do word processing.
   c. Jerry has never done word processing before.

3. a. Paula is a secretary.
   b. Paula is a legal secretary.
   c. Paula has an experienced legal secretary.

4. a. Pete wants to play an electric guitar.
   b. Pete plays an acoustic guitar.
   c. Peter plays an electric guitar.

5. a. Tom has never used a saw before.
   b. Tom doesn't want to learn to use a chain saw because he thinks it's too difficult.
   c. Tom thinks operating a chain saw would be easy to learn.

6. a. Mr. Winston is a wedding photographer.
   b. Mr. Winston is a portrait photographer.
   c. Mr. Winston won't take wedding pictures.

Vocabulary Check: *Word Categories*

Choose the best word to complete the categories below.

e	**1.** change	take in	let out	a.	confident
c	**2.** important	essential	symbolic	b.	certain
g	**3.** tabulator	calculator	adding machine	c.	significant
b	**4.** sure	absolute	positive	d.	manuscript
a	**5.** shy	happy	sad	e.	alter
d	**6.** writing	book	report	f.	projector
f	**7.** camera	screen	movie	g.	cash register

InterAct!

Looking for a Job

Find three wants ads for job openings in the newspaper. Compare your ads with those that other students find. Ask your teacher to help you with any abbreviations you don't understand.

As a class, brainstorm approaches to use when calling for an interview. Practice calling to make an appointment to be interviewed for one of the jobs you found in the newspaper.

With a partner, practice a job interview in which you tell about your skills and abilities. Present the interview to the class. Ask your classmates how effective you were. Then ask them to suggest how you could improve your job interview.

I tried, but the usher wouldn't let me.

save you a seat

(1) disappointed
    upset

(2) What makes you say that?
    Why do you say that?
    Why?
    How come?

(3) I wasn't able to
    I couldn't

(4) The truth is (that)
    The fact of the matter is that

(5) you were counting on me to _____

    you were depending on me
        to _____
    you were expecting me to _____

    you had expected me to _____

A. You're going to be very **disappointed**(1) with me.
B. **What makes you say that?**(2)
A. Well, remember I was supposed to save you a seat?
B. Yes?
A. Well, uh . . . I'm afraid **I wasn't able to**(3) do it.
B. Oh? Why not?
A. **The truth is**(4) I tried, but the usher wouldn't let me.
B. Don't worry about it.
A. I feel bad. After all, **you were counting on me to**(5) save it.
B. Don't worry about it. These things happen.
A. You aren't upset?
B. No, that's okay.

I forgot.

1. fix your doorbell

I got tied up at the office.

2. pick up your dress at the cleaner's

3. buy some groceries on the way home

4. clean the apartment this week

5. get these copied for you

6. get at least a B on my Biology test

7. finish your sweater in time for your birthday

8. get you reservations at the Ritzy Plaza Hotel

9. arrange a blind date for you for Saturday night

Admit to somebody that you weren't able to do something you had said you would do.

25

Function Check: *What's My Line?*

Choose the appropriate line for Speaker B.

	A	**B**
1.	You're going to be very upset with me.	a. I was supposed to be. b. I had promised to. ⓒ How come?
2.	Why couldn't you get the baseball tickets for me?	a. You were counting on me to get them. b. What makes you say that? c. The truth is, they were all sold out.
3.	Have you mowed the lawn yet?	a. Well, I'm afraid I wasn't able to. b. You had expected me to do it. c. No, that's okay.
4.	Do you know how to make French pastries?	a. Yes, I'd like very much to make French pastries. b. Yes, I'm sure. c. Yes, I've had a lot of experience preparing that kind of dessert.
5.	Would you consider yourself an experienced window washer?	a. Washing windows is key. b. Yes, I've had years of experience. c. Yes, I'd be able to.
6.	Remember I was supposed to call Mr. Blaine?	a. That's right. You remember. b. I was supposed to call Mr. Blaine. c. You mean you didn't call him?
7.	The truth is, I don't know how to cook very well.	a. That's okay. b. No, that's all right. c. You're going to be disappointed.
8.	You forgot to return my library books.	a. I know, and you were counting on me to do it. b. That's terrible. Why not? c. I know, and I was counting on you to do it.
9.	Don't worry about the damage you did to our car.	a. I said I would, but I'm sorry. b. But you were counting on me to take care of it! c. What makes you say that?

Listen and choose the answer that is closest in meaning to the sentence you have heard.

1. a. You're going to have an appointment with me.
    b. I'll make it a point to go with you.
    c. You're going to be upset with me.

2. a. I'm going to make a birthday cake for you.
    b. I'm sorry I couldn't make a birthday cake for you.
    c. I'll see if I can make a birthday cake for you.

3. a. Too bad you're moving.
    b. I feel bad that I can't help you study, but I have to move.
    c. I can't help you move because I've got to study.

4. a. My parents are expecting me to baby-sit.
    b. I'm sorry I can't baby-sit for you, but my parents won't allow me to.
    c. My parents can't come to get me when I baby-sit for you.

InterChange

The people on pages 24 and 25 *let others down*. They couldn't do what they had promised. Each one had an excuse.

Which of these excuses do you consider good excuses—legitimate reasons why they couldn't do what they had said they would? Which do you consider *weak* excuses? In your opinion, what could the person have done differently?

InterAct!

How about you? Have you ever *let anyone down*? Have you ever disappointed someone because you weren't able to do something?

What was the situation?
What was the reason?
What did the person say?

With a partner, create a scene depicting the situation and present it to the class.

You have to work a double shift today.

go bowling

my foreman

A. Hi! It's me again!
B. Hi! What up?
A. I'm afraid **I won't be able to**(1) go bowling with you as we had planned.
B. Oh? Why not?
A. My foreman is **insisting that I**(2) work a double shift today, and **there's nothing I can do about it**.(3) I hope you understand.
B. Sure. No problem. **Let's plan on**(4) going bowling some other time.

(1) I won't be able to
    I'm not going to be able to
    I can't

(2) insisting that I
    requiring me to

    [stronger]
    making me
    forcing me to

(3) there's nothing I can do
       about it
    there's no way I can get
       out of it
    I can't get out of it

(4) Let's plan on _____ing
    Let's plan to _____
    We can always _____
    We'll _____

You'd better clean up your room.

my father

1. play tennis

I insist that you stay in bed until your fever breaks.

my doctor

2. have lunch

You have to stay late and help take inventory.

the store manager

3. play racquetball

You need to rerecord three songs.

my producer

4. have dinner

You've got to come to my dance recital!

my little sister

5. go out

Tell a friend why you won't be able to get together.

28

Function Check: *What's the Expression?*

1.

> *Let's _____ visiting the zoo on Sunday.*
> ⓐ plan on
> b. plan to
> c. go

2. There's _____ do about being late to your party.
a. nothing I'll
b. nothing I can
c. no way I can

3. We _____ go cross-country skiing another time.
a. won't be able
b. can't get out of
c. can always

4. My supervisor is _____ go to Texas for a training seminar.
a. insisting that I
b. forcing me
c. requiring me

5. I'm sorry, but I won't _____ go jogging with you this afternoon.
a. plan on
b. going to
c. be able to

6. Does your job _____ wear a tie and jacket?
a. force you
b. require that you
c. insist you to

7. I've just found out that I have to work the night shift, and I _____ out of it.
a. no way can get
b. can't get
c. can't do anything

Grammar Check: *Causative Verbs*

1. I can't leave work early because my boss insists (me to (that I)) work overtime.

2. When I was young, my mother (made me made me to) shine my shoes once a week.

3. My teacher is requiring (me to me) retake the test.

4. The captain of the football team never (let me let that I) play until the last quarter of the game.

5. My lawyer is forcing (that I me to) testify.

6. On my first day of work at the restaurant, they had (me to me) cut 400 carrots for the salad bar!

InterCultural Connections

In Situation 1 on the previous page, the father is insisting that his son clean his room. It is very common for children to have responsibilities at home such as cleaning their rooms and taking out the garbage.

How about in your country? What chores and responsibilities do children typically have at home? What's your opinion of this?

approved by your supervisor

(1) submit
hand in
turn in
give you

(2) You're supposed to
You're required to
You're expected to
You need to
You have to
You've got to
You must
It's necessary for you to
It's required that you

(3) processed
accepted
considered
reviewed
evaluated
acted upon
taken into consideration

(4) required
essential
necessary
mandatory

A. I'd like to **submit**[1] my request for maternity leave.
B. Have you had it approved by your supervisor?
A. Excuse me. Have I had it what?!
B. Approved by your supervisor. **You're supposed to**[2] have your request for maternity leave approved by your supervisor before it can be **processed**.[3]
A. Oh. I haven't done that. I didn't know that was **required**.[4]
B. Oh, yes. It's **essential**.[4]

1. signed by your parents

2. notarized

3. checked by one of our secretaries

4. verified by your physician

5. signed by your spouse

Oh, no! You're submitting a form, but you haven't had it approved.

Listening: *Who's Talking?*

Listen and decide what the relationship between the two speakers is.

1. a. student–student
    b. advisor–advisor
    c. student–secretary ⟵

2. a. student–student
    b. student–doctor
    c. student–university administrator

3. a. telephone company salesperson–customer
    b. police officer–victim
    c. bank officer–customer

4. a. bride–groom
    b. City Hall official–groom
    c. bride–City Hall official

5. a. student–parent
    b. student–school secretary
    c. parent–guidance counselor

6. a. car thief–police officer
    b. driver–car thief
    c. victim–police officer

7. a. manager–manager
    b. customer–travel agent
    c. business executive–secretary

8. a. teacher–parent
    b. teacher–student
    c. parent–child

InterChange

Red Tape!

There are many times in everyday life when we have to deal with bureaucracy—times when we have to go through a lot of *red tape*! These procedures for obtaining permission, approval, or verification of something can seem endless and unnecessary!

Have you ever had this kind of experience? Talk with a partner about a time when YOU had to go through a lot of *red tape*! Then share your experiences with the class.

An employer and a job applicant are talking during a job interview. Practice this scene with a partner.

A. Let me **tell you about**[1] some of our policies and practices here at Globe Insurance.
B. All right.
A. We require all our employees to arrive promptly for work, and we insist that they keep their lunch hours to a reasonable length.
B. I understand.
A. Employee character is very important to us. We expect everyone here at Globe Insurance to be industrious, cooperative, and honest.
B. I'm very glad to hear that.
A. We also try to do the best we can for our employees. We feel obligated to provide a safe working environment, and we make every effort to listen to our employees' concerns.
B. That's very admirable.
A. Now, perhaps you have some questions about working here. Is there any additional information I can provide?
B. Yes, as a matter of fact. I have a few questions.
A. Certainly.
B. Could you tell me whether I would be required to have a medical examination before I start work?
A. Yes, definitely.
B. And would I have to go through special training?
A. Yes, you would.
B. And would it be necessary for me to work weekends?
A. No, that wouldn't be necessary.
B. And one more question: do employees here have to go through a probation period?
A. No, they don't.
B. I see.
A. Do you have any other questions?
B. No, I don't think so.
A. All right.
B. Well, **I've probably taken up enough of your time**.[2] I'll look forward to hearing from you.
A. We'll be in touch with you shortly.
B. **I've enjoyed talking with you.**[3] Thank you very much.
A. You're very welcome.

(1) tell you about
fill you in on
outline for you
advise you of
make you aware of

(2) I've probably taken up
enough of your time.
I don't want to take up any
more of your time.

(3) I've enjoyed talking with
you.
It was nice meeting you.
It was a pleasure meeting
you.
I appreciate this opportunity
to talk with you/meet with
you.

A. Let me **tell you about**(1) some of our policies and practices here at _____.
B. All right.
A. We require all our employees to _____, and we insist that they
_____.
B. I understand.
A. Employee character is very important to us. We expect everyone here at
_____ to be _____, _____, and
_____.
B. I'm very glad to hear that.
A. We also try to do the best we can for our employees. We feel obligated to
_____, and we make every effort to _____.
B. That's very admirable.
A. Now, perhaps you have some questions about working here. Is there any additional
information I can provide?
B. Yes, as a matter of fact. I have a few questions.
A. Certainly.
B. Could you tell me whether I would be required to _____?
A. Yes, definitely.
B. And would I have to _____?
A. Yes, you would.
B. And would it be necessary for me to _____?
A. No, that wouldn't be necessary.
B. And one more question: do employees here have to _____?
A. No, they don't.
B. I see.
A. Do you have any other questions?
B. No, I don't think so.
A. All right.
B. Well, **I've probably taken up enough of your time.**(2) I'll look forward to hearing from you.
A. We'll be in touch with you shortly.
B. **I've enjoyed talking with you.**(3) Thank you very much.
A. You're very welcome.

Now create an original job interview scene with your partner. You can use the model above as a
guide, but feel free to adapt and expand it any way you wish.

Vocabulary Check: *Word Forms*

1.

   Here at Speedy Service Printers we expect our employees to be _____.
   a. prompt
   b. promptly
   c. promptness

2. I think three weeks vacation sounds _____.
   a. reasonably
   b. reason
   c. reasonable

3. All of our construction people are hard-working and _____.
   a. industrial
   b. industry
   c. industrious

4. If you have any _____, we'll be happy to listen to them.
   a. concern
   b. concerned
   c. concerns

5. Mr. Harlow is one of our most _____ workers.
   a. honest
   b. honestly
   c. honesty

6. The _____ period for this job is two weeks.
   a. probe
   b. probation
   c. probing

7. I'm sorry. I've _____ taken up enough of your time.
   a. probable
   b. improbably
   c. probably

8.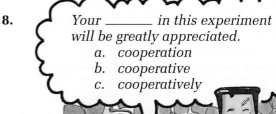

   Your _____ in this experiment will be greatly appreciated.
   a. cooperation
   b. cooperative
   c. cooperatively

Listening: *Conclusions*

Listen and choose the best conclusion.

1. a. This is the beginning of the conversation.
   b. This is the end of the conversation.
   c. Both people have been members of the club for a long time.

2. a. Dr. Young has been working at Memorial Hospital for quite a while.
   b. Dr. Young is just about to leave Memorial Hospital.
   c. Dr. Young is a new intern at Memorial Hospital.

3. a. This is the beginning of the conversation.
   b. Melissa didn't ask any questions about the church.
   c. Melissa is about to leave.

4. a. Jack works for Hamilton Realty.
   b. Dick works for Hamilton Realty.
   c. Jack and Dick both work for Hamilton Realty.

5. a. This is probably the end of the conversation.
   b. Joel knows all about the lab procedures.
   c. Joel doesn't know about the lab procedures.

6. a. Jennifer is about to have a job interview with Mr. Leonard.
   b. Jennifer had never met Mr. Leonard before.
   c. Jennifer is an old friend of Mr. Leonard's.

Years ago when you were looking for a job, you would present yourself at an interview with resume in hand and be hired because you were well groomed, semiqualified, and somewhat experienced. Things have changed in recent years, though. A large number of very qualified people are likely to apply for a desirable position, and in this competitive situation, the impression one makes during an interview can be crucial. Many books and magazine articles are now available to help people compete in this job market and sell themselves to companies,

following many of the same techniques used by advertising agencies to market and sell products.

Printing companies boast about their ability to edit, format, and print quality resumes that will convince employers of their need for you even before you are interviewed. Books on how to *dress for success* give detailed advice.

Other books give advice on how to prepare mentally for an interview, suggesting that you *hire yourself an employer* by taking the initiative in your meeting with the interviewer. Showing that you have done research about the company, demonstrating that your qualifications are appropriate for the position, and persuading an employer that you are the right person for the job are keys to a successful interview. Even if you are not hired, you will have gained valuable knowledge that will come in handy at your next interview.

Job interviews have become an increasingly important part of the U.S. employment scene, not only because of the competition for positions but also because of the growing trend for Americans to have several different jobs during the course of their working years. The rapid rate of technological advance and the expanding and changing economy increase the likelihood that a person will have more than one or two employers in a lifetime. This phenomenon has created the need for many Americans to learn how to *sell themselves* to prospective employers.

In Your Own Words

For Writing and Discussion

What are YOUR ideas for how to *sell yourself* to an employer? What advice do you have for how to write an effective resume and how to *dress for success*?

Write your own *how to* guide. Then compare your ideas with what other students have suggested.

As a class project, select the best ideas and publish a *how to* guide that you can give to other classes in your school.

Here are the expressions you practiced in Chapter 2. Try to use as many as you can to expand your vocabulary and to add variety to your use of English.

Obligation

Inquiring about . . .

Do I have to _____?
Would I have to _____?
Would I be required to _____?
Would it be necessary (for me) to
_____?

Expressing . . .

It's required/necessary/essential/
mandatory.

We require _____ to _____.
We insist (that) _____.
We expect _____ to _____.

You're supposed to _____.
You're required to _____.
You're expected to _____.
You need to _____.
You have to _____.
You've got to _____.
You must _____.
It's necessary for you to _____.
It's required that you _____.

_____ is insisting that I _____.
_____ is requiring me to _____.

[stronger]
_____ is making me _____.
_____ is forcing me to _____.

I didn't know that was required/
essential/necessary/mandatory.

You were counting on me to _____.
You were depending on me to _____.
You were expecting me to _____.
You had expected me to _____.

We feel obligated to _____.

Ability/Inability

Inquiring about . . .

Can you _____?
Are you able to _____?
Do you know how to _____?

You'd consider yourself an
experienced/capable _____?
You'd say you're an experienced/
capable _____?

Expressing Ability

I can (_____).

I'm very good at _____ing.
I've had a lot of experience _____ing.
I've had a good deal of experience
_____ing.
I've had a great deal of experience
_____ing.
I've had years of experience _____ing.

I'm sure/I'm confident/I'm certain/
I know I'd be able to learn quickly.
I'm sure/I'm confident/I'm certain/
I know I could learn quickly.

Expressing Inability

I wasn't able to _____.
I couldn't _____.

I won't be able to _____.
I'm not going to be able to _____.
I can't _____.

I haven't _____ed before.

There's nothing I can do about it.
There's no way I can get out of it.
I can't get out of it.

Denying/Admitting

Admitting

I'm afraid _____.

The truth is (that) _____.
The fact of the matter is (that) _____.

Leave Taking

(Well,) I've probably taken up enough
of your time.
(Well,) I don't want to take up any
more of your time.

I've enjoyed talking with you.
It was nice meeting you.
It was a pleasure meeting you.
I appreciate this opportunity to talk
with you/meet with you.

Remembering/Forgetting

Inquiring about . . .

Remember _____?

Indicating . . .

I forgot.
It (completely) slipped my mind.

Asking for and Reporting Information

What makes you say that?
Why do you say that?
Why?
How come?

What's up?

Perhaps you have some questions
about _____.

I have a few questions.

Could you tell me _____?

I was wondering _____.

I've found out that _____.

Asking for and Reporting Additional Information

Is there any (additional) information I
can provide?
Do you have any (other) questions?

Initiating a Topic

Let me tell you about . . .
Let me fill you in on . . .
Let me outline for you . . .
Let me advise you of . . .
Let me make you aware of . . .

Hesitating

Well, . . .
Well, uh . . .

Initiating Conversations

Hi! It's me again!

Asking for Repetition

Excuse me.

Have I had it what?!

3

REQUESTS 請求

Larry's car won't start. He's asking somebody for a favor. What do you think he's requesting, and how do you think the other person is responding?

Yoshiko's computer isn't working, and she's asking her co-worker Doris for some help. Doris is checking the equipment carefully, but she can't figure out what the problem is. What do you think they're saying to each other?

clean up your room before dinner

(1) Please _____.
Can you (please) _____?
Will you (please) _____?
Would you (please) _____?
I'd like you to _____.
I wish you would _____.

(2) What did you say?
What was that?

(3) Okay.
All right.
Sure.

A. Charlie? **Please**(1) clean up your room before dinner.
B. Sorry, I didn't hear you. **What did you say?**(2)
A. I asked you to clean up your room before dinner.
B. **Okay.**(3)

1. roll up the windows in the car

2. help me fold the laundry

3. change your clothes before our guests arrive

4. take the dog for a walk before you leave for work

5. give me a hand opening this jar of pickles

Ask somebody at home to do something.

retype *the letter to Mr. Casey*
get me the Jones file

(1) Please _____.
Can you (please) _____?
Will you (please) _____?
Would you (please) _____?
I'd like you to _____.
I wish you would _____.

(2) Certainly. /ˈsɜːtənli/
Of course.

A. George? **Please**(1) retype *the letter to Mr. Casey*.
B. The letter to Mr. Casey?
A. Yes. And while you're at it, please get me the Jones file.
B. **Certainly.**(2) I'll do it right away.

1. put these glasses *through the dishwasher*
   get some more spoons and forks

2. take *Mr. Anderson's blood pressure* /blʌd/ /ˈpreʃə/
   check his temperature /ˈtemprɪtʃə/

3. order me *a tuna fish sandwich*
   call my dentist and reschedule my appointment
   /riːˈskedʒuːl/ 重新安排 /əˈpɔɪntmənt/ 预约

IMPORTANT MESSAGE
TO
WHILE YOU WERE OUT

Ask somebody at work to do something.

4. take these boxes *to the stockroom*
   check our supply of glue
   /səˈplaɪ/ /gluː/ 胶水 提供

5. put these fan letters *in my dressing room*
   call NBC and cancel my appearance on "The Today Show"
   /əˈpɪrəns/ 演出

39

Grammar Check: *Reported Speech*

1. A. Can you please turn off the oven for me?
   B. What did you say?
   A. a. I asked if you could turn off the oven for me.
      b. I asked if you had turned off the oven for me.
      c. I asked if you could have turned off the oven for me.

2. A. Please help me make the beds, dear.
   B. What did you ask me to do?
   A. a. I asked you to help me making the beds, dear.
      b. I asked you to help me make the beds, dear.
      c. I asked that you would help me make the beds, dear.

3. A. I wish you would get a job, Stanley.
   B. What was that?
   A. a. I said I wish you would have gotten a job.
      b. I said I wished you would get a job.
      c. I said I have wished you would have gotten a job.

4. A. Larry, I'd like some help cleaning out the garage.
   B. Sorry, grandpa. What did you say?
   A. a. I asked if you could help me clean out the garage.
      b. I asked could you help me clean out the garage.
      c. I asked I'd like some help cleaning out the garage.

5. A. I want you to move your car, Tommy.
   B. Excuse me?
   A. a. I said I had wanted you to move your car.
      b. I said I will want you to move your car.
      c. I said I wanted you to move your car.

6. A. Have you finished your science project yet?
   B. What was that?
   A. a. I wondered whether you had finished your science project.
      b. I wondered have you finished your science project.
      c. I wondered whether you would have finished your science project.

7.
   A. Will you please try not to snore?
   B. What?
   A. a. I asked if you'll try not to snore.
      b. I asked if you won't snore.
      c. I asked if you would try not to snore.

Listening: *Conclusions*

Listen and choose the best conclusion.

1. a. Sally wants George to take the Thompsons out for dinner.
   b. George and Sally are husband and wife.
   c. George doesn't want to take out the garbage.

2. a. Adam's mother wants him to pick up the boys.
   b. Adam's mother wants Adam to pick up his toys by himself.
   c. Adam's mother wants help picking up his toys.

3. a. Rick is in the shower.
   b. The phone is ringing while Frank is in the shower.
   c. Neither Rick nor Frank heard the telephone ringing.

4. a. Mary's father wants Mary and Tom to help unload the dishwasher.
   b. Mary's father wants help unloading the dishwasher.
   c. Mary's father wants Mary to go out with Tom.

5. a. Larry's grandfather wants Larry to help him take out the garbage.
   b. Larry's grandfather wants help cleaning out the garage.
   c. Larry's grandfather is too tired to clean out the garage.

6. a. Alan doesn't want the windows opened.
   b. Betty doesn't want the air conditioning on.
   c. Alan rolled down the windows.

Function Check: *What's the Expression?*

1. Monica, _____ please rewrite this article for me?
   a. you can
   b. I'd like you to
   c. will you *(circled)*

2. Jim, while you're at it, _____ you to pick up some coffee for us, okay?
   a. I'd like
   b. would
   c. I'll like

3. _____, Mrs. Cook, I'll do it immediately.
   a. It's all okay
   b. Certainly
   c. No, thanks

4. Rob, _____ please clean the cat litter?
   a. I wish you would
   b. I'd like you
   c. can you

5. _____ get me some tea, Timothy.
   a. Will you
   b. Please
   c. I'd like you

6. I wish you _____ relax a little.
   a. would
   b. can
   c. please

Listening: *Where Are They?*

Listen and decide where each conversation is taking place.

1. a. in someone's home
   b. at a kitchen supply store
   c. at a shoe store *(circled)*

2. a. at a fish market *(circled)*
   b. at a restaurant
   c. at a furniture store

3. a. in someone's home *(circled)*
   b. in a classroom
   c. in the library

4. a. in the stock room
   b. in someone's home *(circled)*
   c. in an office

5. a. in someone's home
   b. at a copy center *(circled)*
   c. at a gymnasium

6. a. at a supermarket
   b. in a hospital *(circled)*
   c. at a restaurant

InterView

Common Requests

Interview five students in the class about things they are most commonly asked to do. Your interview question might be:

What are the five things your mother/father/wife/husband/boss/teacher most frequently asks you to do?

Report your findings back to the class and compare results.

Could You Do Me a Favor?

give me a lift home

Could you possibly . . . ?

lend me your vacuum cleaner

Would you mind . . . ?

A. **Could you do me a favor?**[1]
B. What is it?
A. **Could you possibly**[2] give me a lift home?
B. **All right.**[3]
A. Are you sure? I don't want to **inconvenience you.**[4]
B. **No problem.**[5] **I'd be happy to.**[6]
A. Thanks. I really appreciate it.

A. **Could I ask you a favor?**[1]
B. What is it?
A. **Would you mind**[2] lending me your vacuum cleaner?
B. **No, I wouldn't mind.**[3]
A. Are you sure? I don't want to **bother you.**[4]
B. **It's no trouble at all.**[5] **I'd be glad to.**[6]
A. Thanks. I really appreciate it.

---

[1] Could you do me a favor?
Could I ask you a favor?
Could you do a favor for me?

---

[2] Could you possibly _____?
Could you (please) _____?
Could I (possibly) ask you to _____?
Would you be willing to _____?
Do you think you'd be able to _____?
I wonder if you could (possibly) _____?

$\longrightarrow$

[3] All right.
Okay.
Sure.
Of course.

Would you mind _____ing?

$\longrightarrow$

No, I wouldn't mind.
No, of course not.
No, not at all.

---

[4] inconvenience you
bother you
trouble you
put you to any trouble
put you out

[5] No problem.
It's no trouble at all.

[6] I'd be happy to.
I'd be glad to.
(It would be) my pleasure.

42

1. Could I ask you to . . .?

2. Would you mind . . .?

3. Would you be willing to . . .?

4. Would you mind . . .?

5. Would you mind . . .?

6. Do you think you'd be able to . . .?

7. I wonder if you could . . .?

Function Check: *What's My Line?*

	A	**B**

1.	Ronnie, would you _____ taking me to the doctor?
	   a. be willing
	   (b.) mind
	   c. possibly
		No. Not at all.

2.	Beth, could you _____ a favor and feed my goldfish while I'm away?
	   a. bother go do
	   b. ask me
	   c. do me
		Sure.

3.	Do you think you _____ be able to pick up my father at the airport?
	   a. could possibly
	   b. would
	   c. would be happy to
		No problem.

4.	No, _____ answering your phone while you're away from your desk.
	   a. I'm not at all
	   b. of course not
	   c. I wouldn't mind
		Thanks. I appreciate it.

5.	Are you sure? I don't want to _____.
	   a. put you out to trouble
	   b. inconvenience
	   c. bother you
		It's no trouble.

6.	I'd be happy to house-sit for you while you're on vacation. It would be _____.
	   a. my pleasure
	   b. my favor
	   c. any trouble at all
		Great! I appreciate it.

7.	John, I _____ if you could possibly hook up my stereo for me this weekend?
	   a. ask you
	   b. wonder
	   c. wish
		Sure. I'd be happy to.

8.	Nancy, could you _____ address these invitations for me?
	   a. mind
	   b. be able to
	   c. possibly
		Of course.

1. Ann said she would be willing ((to design) designing) a poster for the art exhibit.

2. We don't mind (to support   supporting) you as long as you keep trying to find a job.

3. David, could I possibly ask you (to review   reviewing) this book before we add it to our required reading list?

4. Excuse me. Would you mind (to sign   signing) this petition to the governor in support of environmental protection?

5. I'd be happy (to give   giving) you a hand with your math homework.

6. The president asked me (to give   giving) the opening remarks for today's ceremony.

7. You wouldn't mind (to move   moving) to another seat, would you?

8. *Do you think you'd be able (to open   opening) this jar for me? I can't seem to do it.*

InterChange

Asking Favors

Could I ask you a favor?	*Could you do me a favor?*	*Could you do a favor for me?*

Talk with a partner about doing favors for people.

> Tell about favors you've asked people to do.
> Tell about favors people have asked you to do.

> What's the biggest favor you've ever asked anyone to do? Did the person agree to do it?
> What's the biggest favor anyone has asked of you? Did you do it? How did you feel?

InterAct!

Choose one of your personal experiences from above and re-enact it with a partner. Have the class decide whether or not the person asking the favor was *imposing* on the other.

switch seats with me

I was wondering if you'd be willing to . . .?

A. Excuse me. **I was wondering if you'd be willing to**[1] switch seats with me?
B. Switch seats?
A. Uh . . . yes. If you'd be willing to, I'd really appreciate it.
B. **All right.**[2]
A. Thank you very much.
B. **My pleasure.**[3]

*let me off **in front of my house***

Would you mind if I asked you to . . .?

A. Excuse me. **Would you mind if I asked you to**[1] let me off in front of my house?
B. In front of your house?
A. Uh . . . yes. If you'd be willing to, I'd really appreciate it.
B. **No, I wouldn't mind.**[2]
A. Thank you very much.
B. **Don't mention it.**[3]

[1] [less direct, very polite]
I was wondering if you'd (be willing to) _____?
I was wondering if you could possibly _____?
Would you be kind enough to _____?
Could I possibly impose on you to _____?
[more direct, polite]
Could you possibly _____?
Could you (please) _____?
Could I (possibly) ask you to _____?
Would you be willing to _____?
Do you think you'd be able to _____?
I wonder if you could (possibly) _____?

[2] All right.
Okay.
Sure.
⟶ Of course.
I'd be happy to.
I'd be glad to.

[less direct, very polite]
Would you mind if I asked you to _____?
Would I be troubling you (too much) if I asked you to _____?
Would I be imposing on you if I asked you to _____?
[more direct, polite]
Would you mind _____ing?

⟶ No, I wouldn't mind.

[3] My pleasure.   Don't mention it.   (I'm) glad to do it.   You're welcome.

46

1. I was wondering if you'd . . .?

2. Would you mind . . .?

3. Would you be kind enough to . . .?

4. Would I be troubling you too much if I asked you to . . .?

5. Would you be willing to . . .?

6. I wonder if you could . . .?

7. Would I be imposing on you if I asked you to . . .?

Ask if somebody would be willing to do something for you.

Function Check: *What's My Line?*

Choose the appropriate line for Speaker A.

	A	**B**
1.	a. I was wondering if you'd call a taxi for me? b. Would you please call a taxi for me? ⓒ Would you mind if I asked you to call a taxi for me?	No, not at all.
2.	a. Would I be imposing on you if I asked you to mail these packages? b. Would you mind mailing these packages? c. Could you possibly mail these packages?	Sure. It would be my pleasure.
3.	a. Would I be troubling you if I asked you to watch my suitcase? b. Would you be kind enough to watch my suitcase for a minute? c. Would I inconvenience you if I asked you to watch my suitcase?	Of course.
4.	a. Sorry. I don't have time to read your report. b. I'd really appreciate it. c. I'd be happy to read your report.	Thank you.
5.	a. I was wondering if you could possibly keep me company while I drive to New York? b. No, I wouldn't mind. c. No, not at all.	Sure. My pleasure.
6.	a. Thanks so much for offering to help me wallpaper the bathroom. b. Remember, don't wallpaper the bathroom. c. It's no trouble wallpapering the bathroom.	I'm glad to do it.
7.	a. I wouldn't mind moving my car. b. Would I be troubling you too much if I asked you to move your car? c. Would you mind imposing to move your car?	No, I wouldn't mind doing it at all.
8.	a. Would you be kind enough to hold the door open for a minute? b. Would I be imposing on you if I asked you to hold the door open for a minute? c. Am I troubling you to hold the door open for a minute?	Okay.
9.	a. Would you mind working my shift for me this Saturday? b. Could you possibly work my shift for me this Saturday? c. Thank you for working my shift for me this Saturday.	Don't mention it.

1. Greg, _____ if you'd be willing to take my Friday night shift? I've got a date.
   a. I wondered
   b. would you mind
   c. I was wondering ✓

2. Shirley, would you be _____ to look up the details of the Taylor case for me?
   a. imposed
   b. kind enough
   c. troubling

3. Henry, could _____ be responsible for the payroll this month while Martha is on vacation?
   a. you wonder if you'd
   b. I ask you to
   c. you be willing to

4. Don't _____. I'd be happy to help you move.
   a. bother me
   b. mention it
   c. mind

5. Would you _____ lend me your notebook computer for the weekend?
   a. impose if you
   b. possibly if you
   c. be willing to

6. Do you _____ you'd be able to stay this evening to complete the experiment?
   a. think
   b. wonder if
   c. mind if

7. I'd be _____ to fix your flat tire for you.
   a. troubled
   b. imposed upon
   c. glad

8. Louise, would you mind if I _____ to watch the baby for a few hours?
   a. asked you
   b. imposed you
   c. trouble you

9.
   Would I be _____ you if I asked you to take care of my pet snake?
   a. *imposed on*
   b. *imposing*
   c. *troubling*

InterCultural Connections

Situation 5 on page 47 is very common. If friends or family members inform the restaurant that it's someone's birthday, a birthday cake with candles will be brought to the table and the waiters and waitresses will sing *Happy Birthday*.

Is this a custom in your country, too? What other things are done to celebrate someone's birthday in public places and at home?

(1) I'd like to
     I'd love to

(2) I have to
     I've got to
     I need to
     I'm supposed to

(3) I'm (really) sorry.
     I'm awfully sorry.

A. Could I possibly ask you to help me get this refrigerator up the steps?
B. Gee, **I'd like to**,(1) but I'm afraid I can't. **I have to**(2) avoid lifting heavy things.
A. Oh, okay.
B. **I'm really sorry.**(3)
A. Don't worry about it. I understand.

1. Would you be willing to . . .?

2. I wonder if you could . . .?

3. Would you mind . . .?

4. Would you mind if I asked you to . . .?

5. Do you think you'd be able to . . .?

Listening: *The Best Response*

Listen and choose the best response.

1. a. I really appreciate it.
    b. I have to.
    c. Sure. ⓒ

2. a. You're welcome.
    b. No, not at all.
    c. Sure.

3. a. Don't mention it.
    b. I really appreciate it.
    c. I'm sorry. What was that?

4. a. No, of course not.
    b. Sure. No trouble at all.
    c. I'm awfully sorry.

5. a. Sorry.
    b. No trouble at all.
    c. Would you please?

6. a. No, I wouldn't mind.
    b. Sure.
    c. Oh, okay.

Listening: *What's the Meaning?*

Listen and choose the answer that is closest in meaning to the sentence you have heard.

1. a. Would it be possible for me to help you carry those groceries?
    b. Did you ask me to carry those groceries?
    c. Would you please help me carry those groceries? ⓒ

2. a. I'm sorry I can't meet you for tennis this afternoon.
    b. I'm awful at tennis, so I can't help you.
    c. I'm so sorry I can't help you, but I have to play tennis this afternoon.

3. a. I'm afraid I'm on a diet, but I'll try one of your brownies.
    b. I don't mind being on a diet, but I'd rather have one of your brownies.
    c. I wish I could try one of your brownies, but I'm on a diet so I can't.

4. a. I feel sick, so I can't come to your dance performance.
    b. I'm so sorry I can't come to your dance performance, but I'll be away then.
    c. I felt terrible at your dance performance last week, but I went on my business trip anyway.

5. a. I would like to see your slides, but I have to go home and cook dinner.
    b. I stayed to see your slides and cook dinner for your family.
    c. I'd love to stay and see slides of your family, but I have to cook dinner first.

InterChange

I Had to Say No!

Talk with a partner about a time in your life when you had to say "no" to someone.

What was the situation?
Why did you say "no"?
How did the other person react?
How did you feel about it?

Then share your experience with the class. Or, create a scene with your partner based on this experience and present it to the class.

One person is leaving a telephone message, and the other is writing it down. Practice this scene with a partner.

A. Hello. **May I please speak to**[1] Larry?
B. I'm afraid Larry isn't here right now. **Can I take a message?**[2]
A. Yes. This is his friend Bob **calling**.[3] Would you please **ask**[4] Larry to bring a few bottles of soda to the party tonight?
B. Okay. **Just a minute.**[5] I'm writing this down. "Bob called. You should bring a few bottles of soda to the party tonight." Is that it?
A. Yes, I guess so. You might ask him to call me back if he has a chance.
B. All right. I'll give him the message.
A. Thanks very much.
B. Good-bye.
A. Good-bye.

A. Hello. **May I please speak to**[1] _____ ?
B. I'm afraid _____ isn't here right now. **Can I take a message?**[2]
A. Yes. This is _____ **calling**.[3] Would you please **ask**[4]
_____ to _____ ?
B. Okay. **Just a minute.**[5] I'm writing this down. "_____ called. You should
_____ ." Is that it?
A. Yes, I guess so. You might ask him/her to call me back if he/she has a chance.
B. All right. I'll give him/her the message.
A. Thanks very much.
B. Good-bye.
A. Good-bye.

---

[1] May I (please) speak to _____ ?
Can I (please) speak to _____ ?
I'd like to speak to _____ , please.
I'd like to speak to _____ , please, is he's/she's there.
Is _____ there?

[2] Can I take a message?
Can I give him/her a message?
Would you like to leave a message
(for him/her)?

[3] calling
speaking

[4] ask
tell

[5] Just a minute.
Just a moment.
Just one moment.

Now create an original telephone conversation with your partner. You can use the model above as a guide, but feel free to adapt and expand it any way you wish.

> *Hello. This is Susan. I'm not able to answer the phone right now. After the beep, please leave your name and number, and I'll get back to you as soon as I can.*

Nowadays, it is very common to hear messages like this on people's answering machines. Because of the increasing pace of life, irregular work schedules, and away-from-home leisure activities, many people use answering machines so that they don't miss important calls when they are out. Like cassette recorders, answering machines record messages so that when a person arrives home, he or she can simply replay the cassette and find out who has called. Some newer answering machines store messages on a computer chip instead of an audiotape.

Many other ways of relaying messages have been developed out of the need for immediate communication. A little less impersonal than an answering machine is an answering service. For a monthly fee, phone calls can be rerouted to an agency in which a clerk takes down the name, number, and message of the caller. The customer can call the service any time from anywhere and receive messages. Still another way to get phone messages is call-forwarding—rerouting calls to an alternate number, such as one's workplace or health club. A caller dialing a home number automatically reaches another number where the person has forwarded his or her calls.

The fact that telephones are no longer limited to how far the cord will reach is a distinct advantage. Cordless, battery-operated models enable people to carry phones to different rooms of the house and use them in their yards, cars, and boats. Cellular phones with antennas can be installed in cars and are able to transmit calls using a system of transmitters placed throughout a given area. Other cellular phones can be carried anywhere in a small bag, and new models called flip-phones are so small they can fit in your pocket.

Another device is the beeper, so named for the type of signal it emits. Because a beeper fits comfortably into a pocket or on a belt, it is used extensively by people who spend their workday in many different locations, such as medical personnel and home repair people. The beeping signal is heard when a certain number is dialed. People carrying beepers know that they must call somebody back to find out why they were *beeped*.

All these variations on the telephone prove that although a hundred years have passed since its invention, the telephone is still our most important means of personal communication.

In Your Own Words

For Writing and Discussion

Which of these devices are common in your country? Who uses them? Which do YOU have? Tell how you use them in your daily life.

Function Check: *What's My Line?*

Choose the appropriate line for Speaker B.

	A	**B**
1.	How would you like to take a trip to the mountains for the weekend?	a. I have to get going. b. I wasn't able to. ⓒ That sounds like fun.
2.	Would I be required to keep receipts for everything I do on my business trip?	a. No. There's nothing I can do about it. b. No trouble at all. c. Yes. You're expected to.
3.	Kate, could you do me a favor and take notes for me at the science lecture?	a. I can't get out of it. b. Don't mention it. c. Sure.
4.	So, Gloria, you'd consider yourself an experienced pilot?	a. Yes. I've had a great deal of experience flying. b. Yes, I'd love to. c. Certainly. It would be my pleasure.
5.	Judy, we'd like to invite you and Carl to be our guests for dinner this Saturday night.	a. We hope you'll be able to join us. b. We feel obligated to come. c. We'd be delighted to come.
6.	Would you like to leave a message for Mrs. Baker?	a. Do you have any other questions? b. Sorry, I didn't hear you. c. I'm awfully sorry.
7.	Mr. Anthony, before you mail in your taxes, you're required to sign every page.	a. Oh. I really appreciate it. b. Oh. I didn't know that was necessary. c. Oh. I don't want to inconvenience you.
8.	What's up?	a. I've found out that I've been accepted to college. b. Hi! It's me again. c. Let's stay in touch.
9.	Is there any chance you could drop off this package for me at the post office?	a. I'm not sure I can. I've got a class in five minutes. b. No, of course not. c. And while you're at it, please buy me some stamps.

Home work

10.	Well, it's been really nice seeing you again.	a. Yes, I should get going, too. b. Yes, let's get together soon. c. No, I'm not sure I can.
11.	Are you tied up on Thursday?	a. I'd love to. Thanks. b. I'm sorry I have to rush off. c. No, as a matter of fact, I'm free.
12.	Has your request been approved?	a. I'll take that into consideration. b. I haven't submitted it yet. c. It's necessary to have it approved.

Choose the correct expression.

13. Sorry I have to _____ like this.
 a. do a favor for you
 b. rush off
 c. be kind enough

14. Would you by any chance _____ sharing an apartment? I need a roommate.
 a. insists on
 b. be counting on
 c. be interested in

15. I'm _____ I can quickly learn how to repair ten-speed bicycles. I know how to repair three-speed bicycles.
 a. willing to
 b. sure
 c. delighted

16. What _____ that I'll be disappointed?
 a. makes you say
 b. do you say
 c. is essential

17.

_____ make it to the International Dinner next Friday? Everyone we know will be there.
 a. May you
 b. I'd like you to
 c. Can you

18. If you're not _____ tonight, do you think you could go to the concert with me at 7:00?
 a. free
 b. busy
 c. interested

19. Brian, let me _____ in on a few of your new job responsibilities.
 a. fill you
 b. advise you
 c. outline

20. I'd _____ to continue this conversation, but I have a staff meeting in five minutes.
 a. keep in touch
 b. love
 c. call you

21. You _____ by any chance be interested in going canoeing with me next weekend, would you?
 a. won't
 b. would
 c. wouldn't

22.

_Excuse me, but would I be _____ too much if I asked you to move your head?_
 a. requiring you
 b. troubling you
 c. pleasing you

home work

Here are the expressions you practiced in Chapter 3. Try to use as many as you can to expand your vocabulary and to add variety to your use of English.

Requests

Direct, Polite

Please _____.
Can you (please) _____?
Will you (please) _____?
Would you (please) _____?
I'd like you to _____.
I wish you would _____.

And while you're at it, please _____.

Could you do me a favor?
Could I ask you a favor?
Could you do a favor for me?

Would you please ask/tell _____ to
_____?

Direct, More Polite

Could you possibly _____?
Could you (please) _____?
Could I (possibly) ask you to _____?
Would you mind _____ing?
Would you be willing to _____?
Do you think you'd be able to _____?
I wonder if you could (possibly)
_____?

Less Direct, Very Polite

I was wondering if you'd (be willing
to) _____?
I was wondering if you could possibly
_____?
Would you be kind enough to _____?
Would you mind if I asked you to
_____?
Would I be troubling you (too much) if
I asked you to _____?
Could I possibly impose on you to
_____?
Would I be imposing on you if I asked
you to _____?

Responding to Requests

Okay.

All right.
Sure.
Certainly.
Of course.
I'd be happy to.
I'd be glad to.
(It would be) my pleasure.

No, I wouldn't mind.
No, of course not.
No, not at all.
No problem.
It's no trouble at all.

Attracting Attention

Charlie?

Excuse me.

Asking for Repetition

Sorry, I didn't hear you.

What did you say?
What was that?

Gratitude

Expressing . . .

Thanks.
Thanks very much.
Thank you very much.

Responding to . . .

My pleasure.
Don't mention it.
(I'm) glad to do it.
You're welcome.

Appreciation

I really appreciate it.

Initiating Conversations

May I (please) speak to _____?

Can I (please) speak to _____?
I'd like to speak to _____, please.
I'd like to speak to _____, please, if
he's/she's there.
Is _____ there?

Ability/Inability

Expressing Inability

I'd like to/love to, but I'm afraid I
can't.

Obligation

Expressing . . .

I have to _____.
I've got to _____.
I need to _____.
I'm supposed to _____.

Apologizing

I'm (really) sorry.
I'm awfully sorry.

Offering to Do Something

Can I take a message?
Can I give him/her a message?
Would you like to leave a message (for
him/her)?

Checking and Indicating Understanding

Checking One's Own Understanding

The letter to Mr. Casey?

These scenes review the functions and conversation strategies in Chapters 1, 2, and 3. Who do you think these people are? What do you think they're talking about? With other students, improvise conversations based on these scenes and act them out.

1.

2.

3.

4.

5.

6.

7.

8.

4

ADVICE AND SUGGESTIONS

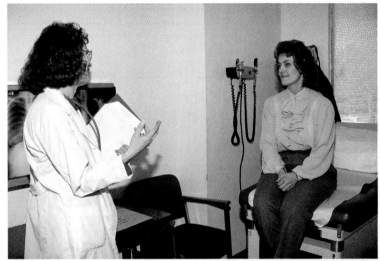

Dr. Smith-Owen is giving her patient, Christine Ferrera, some advice. What do you think she's advising her patient, and how do you think the patient is responding?

The school custodian, Mr. Jenkins, is warning a student to be careful. What do you think he's warning him about? What are they saying to each other?

(1) suggestion(s)
recommendation(s)

(2) How about _____?
What about _____?
I suggest _____.
I'd suggest _____.
I recommend _____.
I'd recommend _____.

(3) Everybody says
Everybody tells me
People say
Most people say
They say
I hear

A. I'm looking for a fresh-tasting toothpaste. Do you have any **suggestions**?(1)
B. A fresh-tasting toothpaste? Hmm. **How about**(2) Tooth-Brite?
A. Tooth-Brite?
B. Yes. I think you'll like it. **Everybody says**(3) it's very fresh-tasting.
A. Okay. Thanks for the **suggestion**.(1)

1.
2.
3.
4.
5.

Ask if somebody has any suggestions.

Function Check: *What's the Expression?*

A

B

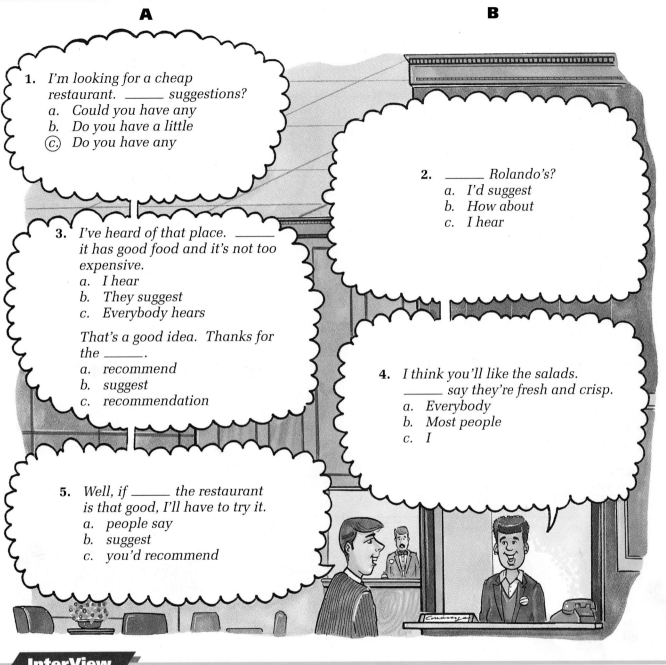

1. I'm looking for a cheap restaurant. _____ suggestions?
   a. Could you have any
   b. Do you have a little
   c. Do you have any

2. _____ Rolando's?
   a. I'd suggest
   b. How about
   c. I hear

3. I've heard of that place. _____ it has good food and it's not too expensive.
   a. I hear
   b. They suggest
   c. Everybody hears

   That's a good idea. Thanks for the _____.
   a. recommend
   b. suggest
   c. recommendation

4. I think you'll like the salads. _____ say they're fresh and crisp.
   a. Everybody
   b. Most people
   c. I

5. Well, if _____ the restaurant is that good, I'll have to try it.
   a. people say
   b. suggest
   c. you'd recommend

InterView

Recommendations

As a class, decide what recommendations you would like to ask other people about. For example:

> What new movies do you recommend?

> What restaurant do you recommend?

Then interview ten people. Ask for their recommendations and the reasons for their recommendations, and report back to the class. Compile the results and see if people in the class agree with the recommendations.

(1) ideas
suggestions
thoughts

(2) How about _____ing?
What about _____ing?
Let's _____.
What if we _____ed?
Why don't we _____?
We could (always) _____.

(3) I don't think I'm in the mood
to _____.
I don't really feel like
_____ing.

(4) Hmm.
[more excited]
Hey!
Say!

(5) Good idea!
That's a/What a good idea!
Good suggestion!
That's a/What a good
suggestion!
That sounds good/great!
That sounds like a good idea!

A. What do you want to do today?
B. I don't know. Do you have any **ideas**?(1)
A. Well . . . **How about**(2) going window-shopping?
B. Oh, I don't know. **I don't think I'm in the mood to**(3) go window-shopping. Any other suggestions?
A. Well, let's see. **What if we**(2) took a ride in the country?
B. **Hmm.**(4) **Good idea!**(5) We haven't taken a ride in the country in ages!

Make a suggestion for doing something today.

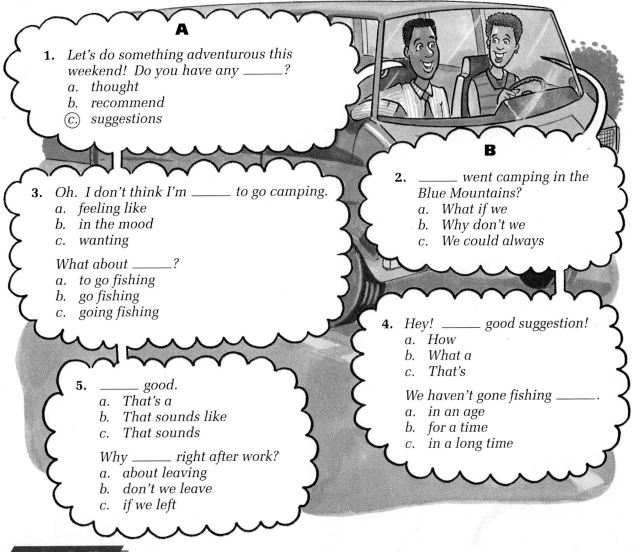

A

1. Let's do something adventurous this weekend! Do you have any _____?
   a. thought
   b. recommend
   ⓒ suggestions

B

2. _____ went camping in the Blue Mountains?
   a. What if we
   b. Why don't we
   c. We could always

3. Oh. I don't think I'm _____ to go camping.
   a. feeling like
   b. in the mood
   c. wanting

   What about _____?
   a. to go fishing
   b. go fishing
   c. going fishing

4. Hey! _____ good suggestion!
   a. How
   b. What a
   c. That's

   We haven't gone fishing _____.
   a. in an age
   b. for a time
   c. in a long time

5. _____ good.
   a. That's a
   b. That sounds like
   c. That sounds

   Why _____ right after work?
   a. about leaving
   b. don't we leave
   c. if we left

InterAct!

The Situation: Act out a conversation in which you are making plans to do something with another student in the class. Choose one of the following emotions and *play the scene* using that emotion:

anxiety   anger   fright   fatigue

surprise   impatience   disgust   boredom

The Challenge: The rest of the class tries to guess what the emotion is!

guidance counselor

take Physics
have trouble getting into medical school

(1) I (strongly) advise you to
    _____.
    I urge you to _____.
    I recommend that you
    _____.
    I recommend _____ing.

(2) important
    necessary

(3) Definitely!
    Absolutely!
    Without question!

(4) you might _____
    you could (possibly)
    _____
    there's a chance you
       might _____
    there's a chance you
       could _____

(5) advice
    suggestion
    recommendation

A. As your guidance counselor, **I strongly advise you to**(1) take Physics.
B. Do you really think that's **important**?(2)
A. **Definitely!**(3) If you don't, **you might**(4) have trouble getting into medical school.
B. Oh. Thank you for the **advice**.(5)

doctor

1. go on a low-fat diet
   have a heart attack some day

lawyer

2. testify in your own defense
   lose your case

dentist

3. brush after every meal
   lose your teeth some day

loan officer

4. take out a smaller loan
   have difficulty meeting the
   monthly payments

stockbroker

5. sell all your shares of Grenomia
   Mining, Limited
   "lose your shirt"

The National Star

Give somebody some strong advice.

64

Check-Up

Function Check: *What's My Line?*

Choose the appropriate line for Speaker B.

	A	**B**
1.	As your insurance broker, I strongly advise you to install a burglar alarm in your car.	a. That might be. b. You could run the risk of having your car stolen. (c.) Do you really think that's necessary?
2.	What course do you advise me to take, Mr. Green?	a. There's a chance you might take Biology. (b.) I recommend that you take Biology. c. I warn you to take Biology.
3.	Do you really think I have to stop doing aerobics every day?	(a.) If you don't, you may permanently injure your back. b. Definitely! I recommend that you do aerobics every day. b. Thanks for the warning.
4.	I recommend taking two aspirin every four hours and drinking a lot of fluids.	a. There's a chance you could catch a cold. (b.) I don't think I'm in the mood. c. Thank you for your advice.
5.	If you don't pay close attention to the signs, you might have trouble finding my house.	a. Absolutely! b. I urge you to drive carefully! (c.) Thanks for the advice.
6.	Do you really think I have to wear a tie and jacket to the interview?	a. You strongly advise me. b. That's advice. (c.) Definitely. If you don't, you might not get the job.

InterChange

Tell about advice different people have given you such as a doctor, a teacher, a parent, or a friend.

Which people gave you advice?
What advice did they give you?
Was it good advice?
Did you listen to them? Why or why not?

I've been having this pain in my chest lately.

see a doctor

(1) You seem troubled/upset.
   You don't seem to be yourself today.

(2) the matter
   wrong
   bothering you

(3) some advice
   a piece of advice
   a suggestion

(4) I think you should/ought to
   _____.
   I/I'd suggest that you
   _____.
   I/I'd suggest _____ing.
   If I were you, I'd _____.
   It seems to me (that) you
      should _____.
   Don't you think you should
      _____?
   Don't you think it might be
      a good idea to _____?

A. **You seem troubled.**(1) Is anything **the matter**?(2)
B. Yes, as a matter of fact. I've been having this pain in my chest lately.
A. Well, can I offer you **some advice**?(3)
B. Sure. What?
A. **I think you should**(4) see a doctor.
B. Hmm. You're probably right.

My old landlord refuses to return my security deposit.

1. take him to court

Bobby Jones has been teasing me all morning.

2. tell the teacher

My supervisor is harassing me.

3. file a complaint through the union

The pressure of this job is "burning me out."

4. take a few days off

I've fallen in love with somebody else, and I don't know how to tell my boyfriend.

5. "level" with him

A friend seems troubled. Give that person some advice.

Function Check: *What's the Expression?*

1. *Maria, you seem _____.*
   a. *yourself*
   b. *upsetting*
   c. *troubled*

2. Is anything _____?
   a. bothered
   b. wrong
   c. mattering

3. Can I offer you _____?
   a. a piece of a suggestion
   b. some of advice
   c. a suggestion

4. I'd suggest _____ to your professor if you want an extension on your paper.
   a. to talk
   b. talking
   c. you should talk

5. _____ you should talk to the boss.
   a. If I were you
   b. It seems to me
   c. Don't think

6. I think you really _____ let Mr. Frank know you're going to be late.
   a. would
   b. ought to
   c. ought

7. Don't you think it _____ be a good idea to call the pediatrician?
   a. might
   b. should
   c. could

8.

   _____, I'd try to get a lot of sleep before your exam tomorrow.
   a. *If you suggest*
   b. *I'd suggest*
   c. *If I were you*

Listening: *The Best Response*

Listen and choose the best response.

1. a. Can I offer you some advice?
   b. Well, I just lost my job.
   c. Sure. What's wrong?

2. a. What's bothering you?
   b. It seems to me that you should.
   c. Okay. What?

3. a. I just had a little accident.
   b. I just heard some good news.
   c. I just got a great job.

4. a. What's bothering you?
   b. Can I offer him a piece of advice?
   c. Yes, he seems troubled.

5. a. Well, I'd suggest calling the police.
   b. What's wrong?
   c. Can I offer him a recommendation?

6. a. I'd suggest that you relax.
   b. Don't you think I should relax?
   c. Yes, that's a good idea.

InterChange

We all have problems in our lives that we could use some good advice about. Here's your chance! Ask members of the class for their advice about a problem you're having. Who knows? They might help you solve your problem!

I've been offered a good full-time job.

put the baby in a child-care center

A. I need your advice on something.
B. Sure. What is it?
A. I've been offered a good full-time job, and I don't know what to do about it.
B. Well . . . **Have you considered**[1] putting the baby in a child-care center?
A. Hmm. **I hadn't thought of that.**[2]

---

[1]
Have you considered _____ing?
Have you thought of _____ing?
Have you thought about _____ing?
Have you given any thought to
    _____ing?
You might consider _____ing.
How about _____ing?

What about _____ing?
Why don't you _____?
You could (always) _____.
It might be a good idea to
    _____.
What if you were to _____?
What if you _____ed?

[2] I hadn't thought
    of that.
That hadn't
    occurred to me.

I'm tired of selling men's underwear.

1. switch to another department

I'm fed up with taking the train to work.

2. form a carpool

3. join "Weight Watchers"

4. ask your landlord to call an exterminator

5. take a semester off

6. get a loan from the bank

7. see a therapist

8. enlist in the armed forces

9. see each other a little less

Ask a friend for some advice about a problem you're having.

	A	**B**
1.	I just found out that repairs on my car are going to cost me $1500.	Have you _____ buying a new car instead of repairing your old one? **a.** given any thought to b. thought to c. considering
2.	I'm sick of getting coffee for the boss!	_____ ask him to get his own coffee? a. How about b. You could **c.** What if you were to
3.	I've been exhausted all week.	_____ sleep late tomorrow. a. Have you thought of b. What about **c.** You could always
4.	I'm fed up with making beds and washing dishes all the time!	You _____ consider sharing the household chores with your family. **a.** should b. don't c. were to
5.	I just can't seem to find someone compatible to go out with.	_____ going to a dating service? a. It might be a good idea **b.** Have you thought of c. You could consider
6.	I'd like to be rich and famous!	Why _____ you buy a lottery ticket? a. don't you consider b. could **c.** don't
7.	Have you thought about talking to your teacher about your problem?	Thanks. I hadn't _____ that idea. a. considering **b.** thought of c. occurred to
8.	My barn is falling apart! I really have to repair it before winter.	You might _____ asking the neighbors to help you fix it. a. think b. always **c.** consider

Grammar Check: *Modals*

1. Karen, you (would (might) ought) consider selling your old furniture so you can afford to buy some new furniture.

2. Mark, I think you (should may can) rest now so that you'll have enough energy for tomorrow's race.

3. It seems to me that Margaret (might not can (ought to)) study harder if she wants to get into an advanced math class next semester.

4. My doctor said that if I didn't take life a little easier, I (would can must) run the risk of having a heart attack.

5. Joe, is there a chance you (could might should) be able to get me some tickets to the concert?

6. If I were you, Mrs. White, I (must should would) be stricter with your children.

7. If you don't clean that cut right away, you (could must should) get an infection.

8.

Brian, don't you think it (might should can) be a good idea to separate the colored laundry from the white laundry?

InterCultural Connections

In the model conversation on page 68, one friend suggests to another that she put her baby in a child-care center while she is at work. What's your opinion of that? In your country, what do working parents do with their children while they are at work? Tell about child-care in your country.

InterChange

I'm tired of . . .!

I'm fed up with . . .!

I've "had it" with . . .!

Do you ever feel this way? Tell students in your class about something that bothers you and see if they have any advice.

get run over

slip

(1) Careful!
Be careful!
Look out!
Watch out!

(2) Huh?

[more polite]
Excuse me?
Pardon me?
Pardon?
I beg your pardon?

(3) Thanks for the warning.
Thanks for warning me.

A. **Careful!**(1)
B. **Huh?**(2)
A. You'd better get out of the way!
B. Oh?
A. That forklift is coming toward you! You might get run over!
B. **Thanks for the warning.**(3)

A. **Be careful!**(1)
B. **Excuse me?**(2)
A. You'd better not walk over there!
B. Oh?
A. The floor is wet! You might slip!
B. **Thanks for warning me.**(3)

1. get hurt

2. get hit

3. get knocked down by a waiter

4. get bitten

5. get fired

Warn somebody about something.

72

Listening: *Where Are They?*

Listen and decide where each conversation is taking place.

1. a. at a waterfall
   b. at the ocean
   c. in a library

2. a. at a natural history museum
   b. at a zoo
   c. in a restaurant

3. a. at an ice cream shop
   b. in a kitchen
   c. at an ice skating rink

4. a. in a classroom
   b. at a swimming pool
   c. at a driving school

5. a. in someone's home
   b. in a hospital
   c. in a classroom

6. a. on top of a building
   b. at the edge of the sidewalk
   c. at a pool

7. a. in an office
   b. in a restaurant
   c. in a library

8. a. in an office
   b. at a construction site
   c. at a baseball game

9. a. at a swimming pool
   b. at a playground
   c. at an airport

InterAct!

Emergency Situations!

Working in small groups, choose one of the following emergency situations, create a scene, and present it to the class.

Several people are relaxing in a park when an elderly person comes down a path and is about to step into a hole. What happens? Can he be warned in time?

Several people are crossing the street at a busy intersection. They see a young girl on a bicycle who is about to ride in front of a fast-moving car! What happens? Can they warn her in time?

Several people are enjoying themselves at the zoo as a young child gets too close to the tiger's cage! What happens? Can he be warned in time?

Several people are riding on a city bus. A woman's purse is wide open! What happens? Can she be warned before a suspicious-looking passenger steals her money?

One friend is asking another for travel recommendations. Practice this scene with a partner.

A. You've been to Paris, haven't you?
B. Yes. As a matter of fact, I used to live in Paris.
A. Well, I'm planning to visit there soon, and I was wondering
    if you could recommend some things to do?
B. Sure. You should definitely go to Notre Dame Cathedral.
    You also ought to see the palace at Versailles. And you must
    visit the Louvre.
A. Those sound like excellent suggestions. Can you
    recommend any good places to eat?
B. Yes. Make it a point to eat at Maxim's. And if you go there,
    I suggest that you order the duck. It's delicious.
A. That sounds good.
B. Oh, and one more thing. Be sure to have someone take your
    picture in front of the Eiffel Tower.
A. I'll do that.
B. Is there anything else I can tell you about?
A. I don't think so. You've been very helpful. Thanks a lot.
B. Send me a postcard, will you?
A. Okay.

A. You've been to _____, haven't you?
B. Yes. As a matter of fact, I used to live in _____.
A. Well, I'm planning to visit there soon, and I was wondering if you could recommend some
    things to do?
B. Sure. You should definitely go to _____. You also ought to see
    _____. And you must visit _____.
A. Those sound like excellent suggestions. Can you recommend any good places to eat?
B. Yes. Make it a point to eat at _____. And if you go there, I suggest that you
    order the _____. It's delicious.
A. That sounds good.
B. Oh, and one more thing. Be sure to have someone take your picture in front of
    _____.
A. I'll do that.
B. Is there anything else I can tell you about?
A. I don't think so. You've been very helpful. Thanks a lot.
B. Send me a postcard, will you?
A. Okay.

You're planning a trip! Create an original scene with your partner and discuss travel recommendations.
You can use the model above as a guide, but feel free to adapt and expand it any way you wish.

Advertising in the United States dates back to 1704, when the first paid ads were printed in early colonial newspapers. Since then, advertising has developed into a major industry. Why has it grown to be such an important force in U.S. society? What effect does it have on the minds of consumers and the decisions they make? A look at different types of advertising may shed some light on these questions.

One type of advertising is intended only to create an *image* of a product in the minds of the public. This type of advertising has long-range goals and takes place over a long period of time. Another type of advertising creates an *awareness* of a new product or changes in an existing one and runs over a shorter time period. The last type is the most common—advertising that encourages *immediate action*. This includes ads for items at bargain prices and for other types of special offers that lead to increased sales.

Vast amounts of television and radio time and large portions of newspaper and magazine space are devoted to advertising. This bombardment of words and images proclaiming that every product is the best leads some people to believe that much of what they see or hear is not true. For example,

few people outside of advertising would describe a soft drink as "cool, crisp, light, and refreshing" or claim that a toothpaste is the main reason they fell in love with someone. Such exaggeration makes many people doubt the claims advertisements make about a product. Actual misrepresentation of facts, however, is very rare. Consumer groups study products and keep the public informed of their good and bad qualities.

In a way, advertising provides a valuable service to the public. It calls people's attention to products and services, and it contributes to the dynamic marketplace in which companies compete for the attention and loyalty of consumers who are ever on the lookout for something new or better.

In Your Own Words

Find advertisements in newspapers, magazines, on television, and on radio that are examples of the three types described above—those that create an image, those that promote awareness, and those that encourage immediate action.

Now create your own ads! Using an existing product or one that you invent, create three different advertisements for the same product—one for each type of ad.

Image

What kind of product is X?
What kind of people use it?
What will others think of you if you use X?
How will you feel if you use X?

Awareness

What features does X have?
What can X do?
What can you do if you use X?
X is better than other products because . . .

Immediate Action

X usually costs . . .
Now it costs only . . .
This special offer is good only until . . .

Here are the expressions you practiced in Chapter 4.   Try to use as many as you can to expand your vocabulary and to add variety to your use of English.

Advice–Suggestions

Asking for . . .

I need your advice on something.

Do you have any suggestions/
   recommendations/ideas/thoughts?

Can you recommend _____?
I was wondering if you could
   recommend _____?

Any other suggestions?

Offering . . .

Can I offer you { some advice?
a piece of advice?
a suggestion?

I (strongly) advise you to _____.
I urge you to _____.
I recommend that you _____.
I recommend _____ing.

You should (definitely) _____.
You ought to _____.
You must _____.
Make it a point to _____.
Be sure to _____.

I think you should/ought to _____.
I/I'd suggest that you _____.
I/I'd suggest _____ing.
If I were you, I'd _____.
It seems to me (that) you should _____.
Don't you think you should _____?
Don't you think it might be a good
   idea to _____?

How about _____?
What about _____?
I suggest _____.
I'd suggest _____.
I recommend _____.
I'd recommend _____.

How about _____ing?
What about _____ing?
Let's _____.
What if we _____ed?

Why don't we _____?
We could (always) _____.

Have you considered _____ing?
Have you thought of/about _____ing?
Have you given any thought to
   _____ing?

You might consider _____ing.
How about _____ing?
What about _____ing?
Why don't you _____?
You could (always) _____.
It might be a good idea to _____.
What if you were to _____?
What if you _____ed?

Responding to . . .

Good idea!
That's a/What a good idea!
Good suggestion!
That's a/What a good suggestion!
That sounds good/great!
That sounds like a good idea!

I hadn't thought of that.
That hadn't occurred to me.

Warning

If you don't (_____), _____.

Careful!
Be careful!
Look out!
Watch out!

(You'd better) *get out of the way!*
(You'd better) stay away from the
   _____!
(You'd better) keep clear of the _____!
You'd better not _____!
Don't _____!

You might _____.

Gratitude

Expressing . . .

Thanks/Thank you for _____.

Thanks a lot.

Want-Desire

Inquiring about . . .

What do you want to do today?

Expressing . . .

I don't think I'm in the mood to _____.
I don't really feel like _____ing.

Possibility/Impossibility

Expressing . . .

You might _____.
You could (possibly) _____.
There's a chance you might _____.
There's a chance you could _____.

Asking for and Reporting Information

Is anything { the matter?
wrong?
bothering you?

Everybody says . . .
Everybody tells me . . .
People say . . .
Most people say . . .
They say . . .
I hear . . .

Asking for Repetition

Huh?

[more polite]
Excuse me?
Pardon me?
Pardon.
I beg your pardon?

Hesitating

Hmm.
Well, . . .
(Well,) let's see . . .

Initiating a Topic

You seem troubled/upset.
You don't seem to be yourself today.

Checking and Indicating Understanding

Checking One's Own Understanding

Tooth-Brite?

5

AGREEMENT AND DISAGREEMENT
DENYING AND ADMITTING
CORRECTING

Jessica and Rithy agree about the food in their school cafeteria. What do you think they're saying to each other?

Leslie is accusing her brother Keith of doing something, and Keith is denying it. What do you think they're saying to each other?

We had a very good fourth quarter.

(1) I agree.
I agree with you.
You're right.
That's right.
That's true.
I know.

(2) Absolutely!
Definitely!

A. We had a very good fourth quarter.
B. **I agree.**(1) We DID have a very good fourth quarter, didn't we.
A. **Absolutely!**(2)

Business is lousy tonight.

1.

It looks like it's going to rain.

2.

The students gave a wonderful performance today.

3.

George was a kind and generous person.

GEORGE WILSON

4.

This is a GIGANTIC wisdom tooth!

5.

Agree with somebody.

- *That was a terrible movie!*
- *The acting was awful!*
- *And the storyline was impossible to follow!*

CINEMA
NOW SHOWING
THE BIG SHOT

(1) I agree.
You're right.
I know.

[less formal]
I'll say!

(2) That's just what I was thinking.
That's exactly what I was thinking.
I couldn't agree with you more.
I feel the same way.
That's exactly what I think.
My feelings exactly.

[less formal]
You can say that again!
You took the words right out of my mouth!

A. That was a terrible movie!
B. It was.
A. The acting was awful!
B. **I agree.**(1)
A. And the storyline was impossible to follow!
B. **That's just what I was thinking.**(2)

- *She's an awful singer!*
- *Her voice is so loud!*
- *And she's singing off key!*

1.

- *Mr. and Mrs. Wagner have such wonderful children!*
- *They're very well mannered!*
- *And they're so friendly to everybody in the neighborhood!*

2.

- *This bus driver drives like a maniac!*
- *He's constantly changing lanes!*
- *And he's traveling much too fast!*

3.

- *Walter made a food of himself at the party!*
- *He ate all the desserts.*
- *And he told the same "corny" jokes he's been telling for years!*

4.

- *Dr. Frankenstein has been acting very strangely recently!*
- *He's very nasty to everybody in the village!*
- *And I bet he's up to something in his laboratory.*

5.

Agree with somebody about several things.

Grammar Check: *Tag Questions*

1. You're not going to leave now, _____?
   a. are you going to
   b. will you
   c. (are you)

2. Dr. Patrick didn't have a very good bedside manner, _____.
   a. had he
   b. (did he)
   c. does he

3. It's true that Marcia is going to be transferred to Saudi Arabia, _____?
   a. is she
   b. won't she
   c. (isn't it)

4. Your lawyer isn't making you testify, _____?
   a. isn't she
   b. (is he)
   c. are you

5. It looks like the Dodgers are going to win the baseball game, _____.
   a. are they
   b. (doesn't it)
   c. will they

6. We've had a wonderful evening, _____.
   a. (haven't we)
   b. hadn't we
   c. didn't we

7. You wouldn't want to go now, _____?
   a. would we
   b. do you
   c. (would you)

8. Mrs. McDonald's a brilliant philosophy teacher, _____.
   a. wasn't she
   b. isn't she
   c. hasn't she

Grammar Check: *Adjectives and Adverbs*

1. The painters did an ((awful) awfully) job painting the living room.

2. Most of the amateur singers we heard at the tryouts today sang (off-key off-keyly).

3. That was a (lousy lousily) movie we saw last night, wasn't it.

4. I am (constant constantly) reminding him to balance his checkbook, but he hasn't done it yet.

5. The chairman of the board gave an (inspiring inspiringly) speech last week.

6. Betsy is a very (well mannered well mannerly) student.

7. Uncle Ralph is always telling (corny cornily) jokes.

8. I can't believe how (wonderful (wonderfully)) your son plays the trombone, Mrs. Martinetti!

9. I give up! This math problem is ((impossible) impossibly) to solve!

10. Everybody in the community admired your husband, Mrs. Harrison! He gave (generous (generously)) to so many charities!

11. David, you did a (remarkable remarkably) job on your science project!

12. My cat was behaving a little (strange strangely) last night after she ate. Maybe she's sick.

Function Check: *What's My Line?*

Choose the appropriate line for Speaker B.

	A		**B**
1.	That was a wild rock concert!	a. b. c.	My feelings! You can say! You're right! (circled)
2.	How foolish we were when we were young!	a. b. c.	I'll say! (circled) That's exactly! I know what I think.
3.	That poetry reading was wonderful!	a. b. c.	I couldn't agree the same way. I agree. (circled) You took the words out.
4.	That was the most exciting trapeze act I've ever seen!	a. b. c.	What a way to think! My feelings! My feelings exactly. (circled)
5.	This chocolate souffle is exquisite!	a. b. c.	It isn't. You couldn't feel the same way. I know. (circled)
6.	Can you believe it's Sunday night already? Vacations are always too short!	a. b. c.	You took the words right out of my mouth! (circled) Your feelings exactly! I feel you're right!

InterView

Make a list of ten opinions you have. They can be about anything you wish. For example:

I think the president is doing a wonderful job.

In my opinion, Tooth-Brite is the best toothpaste.

Walk around the room asking different students what they think. Try to find someone who agrees with ALL ten of your opinions.

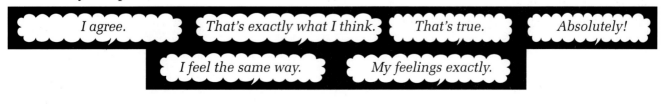

I agree. *That's exactly what I think.* *That's true.* *Absolutely!*

I feel the same way. *My feelings exactly.*

(1) That might be true.
That may be true.
You might be right.
You may be right.
You have a point (there).
I see your point.
I know.

(2) Wouldn't you agree (that)
Wouldn't you say (that)
Don't you think (that)

(3) I suppose you're right.
I guess you're right.
I suppose that's true.
I guess that's true.

A. This car is a very old model!
B. **That might be true.**(1) However, . . . **wouldn't you agree that**(2) it's in excellent condition?
A. Hmm. **I suppose you're right.**(3)

1.
2.
3.
4.
5.

Respond to somebody's opinion with an opposite point of view.

(1) I'm afraid you're right.
I hate to admit it, but
  you're right.
I hate to say it, but you're
  right.

(2) It's true.
Absolutely!
Definitely!
No doubt about it!

[less formal]
I'll say!

A. You know . . . I've noticed that you've been very quiet recently.
B. **I'm afraid you're right.**(1) I HAVE been very quiet recently, haven't I.
A. **It's true.**(2)

1.

2.

3.

4.

5.

Reluctantly agree with somebody.

Function Check: *What's My Line?*

Choose the appropriate line for Speaker B.

	A		**B**
1.	This stereo has good sound, but wouldn't you agree that it's too expensive?	a. b. c.	I suppose I know. I guess that's true. I guess that's a point.
2.	Don't you think that pink and yellow tie is a little too wild to wear to work?	a. b. c.	You have a point there. I suppose you'd say that. You don't have a point.
3.	Martin has a terrible singing voice, doesn't he?	a. b. c.	Yes, but he sings off-key. That might be true, but he plays the guitar beautifully. Wouldn't you say that?
4.	Our hockey team is the best one in the state.	a. b. c.	However, don't you think that my team is better? I suppose my team is better. That may be true, but my team beat yours in the state championship.
5.	Mr. Jones is a strict teacher, but the students learn a lot from him.	a. b. c.	I know. Maybe true. I see you know.
6.	Wouldn't you say that Tom's house needs a paint job?	a. b. c.	Don't think that. You have a point, but I think it looks great anyway. I suppose you should be right.
7.	I think this neighborhood is really deteriorating.	a. b. c.	I see the point. However, that may be true. I guess you're right.
8.	The air in this city is so polluted!	a. b. c.	But don't you think it's a beautiful city anyway? That may be a point. However, don't you think you're right?

84

Listening: *Positive or Negative?*

Listen and decide whether the speakers agree on a positive or negative opinion.

1. a. positive
    b. negative ⃝

2. a. positive
    b. negative

3. a. positive
    b. negative

4. a. positive
    b. negative

5. a. positive
    b. negative

6. a. positive
    b. negative

7. a. positive
    b. negative

8. a. positive
    b. negative

9. a. positive
    b. negative

Listening: *What's the Meaning?*

Listen and choose the answer that is closest in meaning to the sentence you have heard.

1. a. I'm afraid I've been fired.
    b. You've been noticeably tired recently. ⃝
    c. I got a notice that you've been fired.

2. a. I hate to say it, but I've missed ten classes.
    b. I hate to say it, but my attention in class hasn't been very good lately. ⃝
    c. I had to be admitted to school late because I couldn't attend the first two classes.

3. a. It's true. Joe is getting better grades this semester. ⃝
    b. Absolutely! Joe isn't really improving his grades this semester.
    c. That's right. Joe's sister is really improving.

4. a. I'll say! There are a lot more people at the lake this year than there were last year. ⃝
    b. I'm afraid the lake is too crowded.
    c. No doubt about it. The crowd last year was bigger.

5. a. It's true. I really am going to the ball.
    b. I'd love to stay, but it's true I have to go.
    c. I hate to say it, but I really am losing my hair. ⃝

6. a. It's true. The boss has been working.
    b. Definitely. The boss has been doing strange things at work. ⃝
    c. Don't shout about it! The fact of the matter is the boss is working.

[handwritten notes:] doubt — dout   I doubt it   I don't think so   No doubt about it

InterChange

As a class, talk about the city or town where you live. Tell about the advantages as well as the disadvantages.

> *Our public transportation system is excellent.*
>
> *That may be true, but our taxes are too high.*
>
> *You know, our neighborhoods aren't as safe as they were a few years ago.*
>
> *I'm afraid you're right.*

As a class, give an honest evaluation of your city or town and how it compares to other places you know.

That Isn't Exactly Right

The bread goes in aisle four.

Aisle FIVE

Excuse me, Mr. Perkins . . .

(1) that isn't exactly right
that isn't quite right
that isn't exactly correct
that isn't quite correct
that (really) isn't so
I think you might be mistaken

(2) Thank you for calling that to
   my attention.
Thank you for correcting me
   (on that).

A. The bread goes in aisle four.
B. Excuse me, Mr. Perkins, but **that isn't exactly right.**(1)
A. Oh?
B. Yes, Mr. Perkins. Actually, the bread goes in aisle FIVE.
A. Oh. **Thank you for calling that to my attention.**(2)

Our special tonight is baked chicken.

BROILED FISH

1. Excuse me, Mrs. Alfredo, . . .

Our stock went up ten points today!

DOWN ten points

2. Excuse me, Mr. Jordan, . . .

Children's Clothing is on the third floor.

on the SECOND floor

3. Excuse me, Ms. Whitehead, . . .

I see we're going to remove your appendix tomorrow.

remove my TONSILS

4. Excuse me, Doctor, . . .

I just had a very cordial and successful meeting with the ambassador from Sweden.

the ambassador from SWITZERLAND

5. Excuse me, Mr. President, . . .

IMPORTANT MESSAGE
TO
WHILE YOU WERE OUT

Politely disagree with a superior.

Function Check: *What's My Line?*

	A	**B**

1.	Those armchairs go on the fourth floor, Jack.	Excuse me, Mrs. Smith, but that isn't _____. They go on the FIFTH floor.
		   a. quite
		   b. mistaken
		   (c.) exactly right

2.	Well, Mr. Williams, your car is fixed, but you need a new radiator.	Thank you for _____, Mike.
		   a. calling my attention
		   b. attending that
		   c. calling that to my attention

3.	The population of the bald eagle has increased sharply over the past decade.	Excuse me, Professor Jones, but I think _____. Hasn't the population DECREASED lately?
		   a. that isn't so correct
		   b. you might be mistaken
		   c. you're exactly wrong

4.	I hate to say this, Mr. Albert, but you misspelled my name.	Oh. Thank you for _____ on that.
		   a. correcting me
		   b. calling
		   c. paying attention to me

Listening: *Conclusions*

Listen and choose the best conclusion.

1. a. Pete thinks the temperature is going to be 17 degrees.
    b. Bob heard a different weather report on TV.
    (c.) Bob thinks the temperature is going to be higher than 70 degrees.

2. a. John wrote the song in 1968.
    b. Kathy thought the Beatles wrote the song in 1969.
    c. The Beatles wrote the song in 1969.

3. a. George is growing a beard.
    b. Ron forgot to shave this morning.
    c. George forgot to shave this morning.

4. a. Bertha is celebrating her birthday today.
    b. Bertha's ninety-second birthday is tomorrow.
    c. Bertha will be ninety-one tomorrow.

5. a. The safe deposit vault is open daily.
    b. The safe deposit vault is open from 9:00 A.M. to 2:00 P.M. every day.
    c. The safe deposit vault is open after 3:00 P.M. every day.

In Your Own Words

Write down as many facts as you can think of about different students in your class, but change one small detail for each fact. Share your *incorrect* facts with the class, and the students will correct you . . . politely, of course!

(1) That's not true!
That's wrong!
You're wrong!
You're mistaken!
That (just) isn't so!

(2) Come on!
Look!
Listen!

(3) Admit it!
Face it!

(4) I know
I'm sure
I'm positive
I'm convinced

A. You've been reading my boyfriend's letters, haven't you.
B. **That's not true!**(1)
A. **Come on!**(2) **Admit it!**(3) **I know**(4) you have.
B. That just isn't so. I HAVEN'T been reading his letters!

1. You're scared, . . .

2. Your parents don't approve of me, . . .

3. You want to beak up with me, . . .   ~break~

4. You don't like my meatloaf, . . .

5. You murdered Mrs. Winston, . . .

Strongly deny somebody's accusation.

Function Check: *What's My Line?*

Choose the appropriate line for Speaker B.

	A		**B**
1.	You're angry with me, aren't you.	a. b. c.	Admit it! I'm sure. That's not true.
2.	You're wrong. I didn't cheat on the exam.	a. b. c.	Come on! I know you did. That's wrong. I'm convinced.
3.	You've been procrastinating again, haven't you.	a. b. c.	No, that's not true. Face it! Listen!
4.	I promise! I haven't been sneaking cookies from the cookie jar!	a. b. c.	Look! I know you have! Come on! You're mistaken! Listen! That's true.
5.	The police officer gave me only a warning instead of a ticket because I reasoned with her.	a. b. c.	You're not sure. I'm not so sure I believe that! That's not positive.

In row 1, option c. "That's not true." is circled.

Grammar Check: *Short Answers*

1. My husband thinks the construction workers are never going to finish on time, but I (will   won't   (do)).

2. I'm convinced the veterinarian did everything he could for the dog, but my children are convinced he (could   didn't   couldn't).

3. I'm beginning to think Sam doesn't want to work for us anymore. I just know he (doesn't   isn't   can't).

4. My wife is convinced that Herbert's promotion won't affect my job, but I'm positive it (won't   didn't   will).

5. The rental agency claims this car was in perfect condition when I took it, but they're mistaken. It (isn't   wasn't   didn't).

Has anybody ever wrongly accused you of something you didn't do? What did the person think? Why? How did you feel?

Two people with very different opinions about an issue are disagreeing. Practice this scene with a partner.

A. **Don't you think that**[1] somebody should do something about all the violence on children's cartoon programs?

B. Well . . . **I'm not so sure about that.**[2]

A. Oh?

B. Yes. **I wish I could agree with you,**[3] but **if you ask me,**[4] kids aren't very affected by what they see on TV because they know it isn't real.

A. Well . . . **I disagree.**[5]

[1] Don't you think (that) Wouldn't you say (that) Wouldn't you agree that	[2] I'm not so sure (about that). I don't know (about that). I'm not sure I agree (with you on that). I wouldn't say that. I wouldn't go as far as that. I wouldn't go so far as to say that.	[3] I wish I could agree (with you) I hate to disagree (with you) I don't mean to disagree (with you) I don't want to argue (with you) (about that) I don't want to get into an argument (with you) (about that)

[4] if you ask me, in my opinion, as far as I'm concerned,	I personally think, as I see it, the way I see it,	[5] I disagree. I don't agree. I can't agree. I don't think so.

Now create original scenes with your partner based on the situations below. You can use the model on page 88 as a guide, but feel free to adapt and expand it any way you wish.

Now have a disagreement with somebody else about another issue!

Function Check: *What's the Expression?*

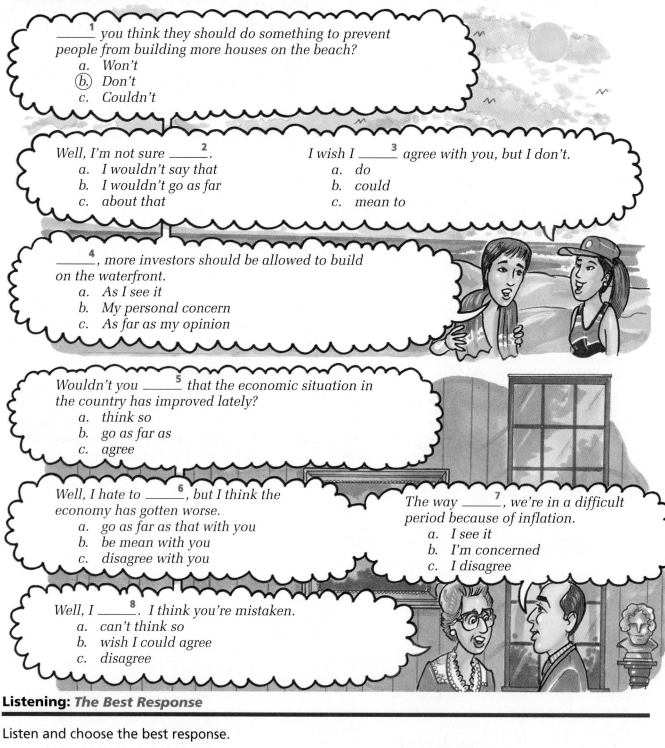

_____ ¹ you think they should do something to prevent people from building more houses on the beach?
- a. Won't
- (b.) Don't
- c. Couldn't

Well, I'm not sure _____ ².
- a. I wouldn't say that
- b. I wouldn't go as far
- c. about that

I wish I _____ ³ agree with you, but I don't.
- a. do
- b. could
- c. mean to

_____ ⁴, more investors should be allowed to build on the waterfront.
- a. As I see it
- b. My personal concern
- c. As far as my opinion

Wouldn't you _____ ⁵ that the economic situation in the country has improved lately?
- a. think so
- b. go as far as
- c. agree

Well, I hate to _____ ⁶, but I think the economy has gotten worse.
- a. go as far as that with you
- b. be mean with you
- c. disagree with you

The way _____ ⁷, we're in a difficult period because of inflation.
- a. I see it
- b. I'm concerned
- c. I disagree

Well, I _____ ⁸. I think you're mistaken.
- a. can't think so
- b. wish I could agree
- c. disagree

Listening: *The Best Response*

Listen and choose the best response.

1.
- a. Well, I really wouldn't say.
- b. I'm afraid you're right.
- (c.) Well, I'm not so sure I agree with you.

2.
- a. I hate to disagree with you.
- b. Oh, I wouldn't say that.
- c. If you ask me, I'm positive.

3.
- a. Wouldn't you agree?
- b. I don't want to start an argument with you, but I disagree.
- c. If you ask me, I hate to disagree.

4.
- a. I hate to argue.
- b. Wouldn't you agree?
- c. You're right.

Good management has always been valued at the workplace. As early as the end of the nineteenth century, studies to improve the efficiency of industrial plants were being conducted. The emphasis, however, was usually on increasing production mechanically. It was not until the latter half of the twentieth century that importance was given to increasing production in other ways.

One of the reasons that businesses started taking another look at management was that the post–World War II boom had ended. The oil crisis early in the 1970s caused prices to rise and markets to shrink. A survey of international economies revealed that Japan, which had been at the bottom of the ladder immediately after the war, was now rapidly climbing to the top. Experts began to study the Japanese style of management in hopes of being able to transfer some of its practices to U.S. companies.

The result was the formulation of several theories of management, which have been termed theories X, Y, and Z. Theory X reflects the traditional view of the boss-worker relationship. It states that, basically, people do not like to work. They perform their jobs because they need the money and they are afraid of being fired. Theory Y is based on the idea that people do like to work. Given good working conditions and enough responsibility, they will find satisfaction in even the most menial tasks.

Theory Z describes the approach to management common in Japan. According to this theory, workers perform most effectively when they take part in the decision-making process and are ultimately responsible for the performance of their group or division. The format for this employee participation, often referred to as quality circles, is becoming increasingly common in workplaces in other countries as a means of improving employee morale and productivity.

The transfer of management styles from one country or setting to another, however, is not always feasible or desirable. An examination of successful companies in the United States reveals special traits unique to American business practices. Among them are *suggestion boxes* or the practice of letting workers or customers contribute new ideas or constructive criticism in order to improve a product or system. *Focus groups* are meetings of company officials to which workers and customers are invited to discuss certain issues and give their opinions on them. Many U.S. companies encourage entrepreneurship. Individuals or groups are provided with the time and facilities to work on a new product or idea without having to leave the company. Monetary incentives, such as profit sharing and stock options, enable employees to share in the company's financial gains.

What Do They Mean?

What do you think these expressions in the reading mean?

1. "the post–World War II boom" (second paragraph)
2. "at the bottom of the ladder" (second paragraph)
3. "menial tasks" (third paragraph)
4. "employee morale and productivity" (fourth paragraph)

In Your Own Words

You are the manager of the newly formed ABC Company. Your employees have just presented you with these complaints and suggestions.

1. The 30-minute lunch break is too short. We would like an hour.

2. We would like vending machines for soda and snacks installed in our work area so we don't have to go all the way to the cafeteria during coffee breaks.

3. We think that we deserve a bonus at the end of the year. Most employees in other companies are given one.

Write a memo to your employees, responding to their concerns.

Here are the expressions you practiced in Chapter 5. Try to use as many as you can to expand your vocabulary and to add variety to your use of English.

Agreement/Disagreement

Inquiring about . . .

Wouldn't you agree (that) _____?
Wouldn't you say (that) _____?
Don't you think (that) _____?

Expressing Agreement

I agree.
I agree with you.
You're right.
That's right.
That's true.
It's true.
I know.

Absolutely!
Definitely!
No doubt about it!

[less formal]
I'll say!

That's just what I was thinking.
That's exactly what I was thinking.
I couldn't agree with you more.
I feel the same way.
That's exactly what I think.
My feelings exactly.

[less formal]
You can say that again!
You took the words right out of my mouth!

I suppose you're right.
I guess you're right.
I suppose that's true.
I guess that's true.

That might be true.
That may be true.
You might be right.
You may be right.
You have a point (there).
I see your point.
I know.

Expressing Disagreement

I disagree.
I don't agree.
I can't agree.

I don't think so.
I'm not so sure (about that).
I don't know (about that).
I wouldn't go as far as that.
I wouldn't go so far as to say that.
I wish I could agree (with you), but . . .
I hate to disagree (with you), but . . .
I don't mean to disagree (with you), but . . .
I don't want to argue (with you) (about that), but . . .
I don't want to get into an argument (with you) (about that), but . . .

Wouldn't you agree (that) _____?
Wouldn't you say (that) _____?
Don't you think (that) _____?

Correcting

Giving Correction

That isn't exactly right.
That isn't quite right.
That isn't exactly correct.
That isn't quite correct.
That (really) isn't so.
I think you might be mistaken.

(Actually,) *the bread goes in aisle FIVE.*
That just isn't so. *I DO like your meatloaf.*

Responding to Correction

Thank you for calling that to my attention.
Thank you for correcting me on that.

Certainty/Uncertainty

Expressing . . .

I know _____.
I'm sure _____.
I'm positive _____.
I'm convinced _____.

Initiating a Topic

You know, . . .

Don't you think (that) _____?
Wouldn't you say (that _____?
Wouldn't you agree (that) _____?

Denying/Admitting

Denying

That's not true!
That's wrong!
You're wrong!
You're mistaken!
That (just) isn't so!

Admitting

I'm afraid you're right.
I hate to admit it, but you're right.
I hate to say it, but you're right.

Persuading–Insisting

Come on!
Look!
Listen!

Admit it!
Face it!

Focusing Attention

If you ask me, . . .
In my opinion, . . .
As far as I'm concerned, . . .
I personally think . . .
As I see it, . . .
The way I see it . . .

6

POSSIBILITY AND PROBABILITY
CERTAINTY AND UNCERTAINTY

Dorothy Harris is worried because it's late and her daughter isn't home yet. She's sure something must have happened. She's thinking about all the things that might have caused her daughter to be late. What do you think she's thinking to herself?

Walter Perkins has just brought his car in for repairs. He's describing the problem to the mechanic, and the mechanic is telling him what's probably wrong with the car, how much it will probably cost to repair it, and when it is likely to be ready. What do you think they're saying to each other?

A. Do you want to go through with this?
B. Yes, I do.
A. Are you **certain**?[1]
B. **I'm positive.**[2] **I definitely**[3] want to go through with this.

A. Is it going to rain?
B. No, it isn't.
A. Are you **sure**?[1]
B. **Absolutely!**[2] **There's no chance**[4] it's going to rain.

[1] certain
sure
positive

[2] I'm positive/certain/sure.
I'm absolutely positive/
certain/sure.
Absolutely!
Positively!

[3] I definitely
There's no question
(in my mind) I
I have no doubt (at all)
that I

[4] There's no chance (that)
There's no possibility
(that)

[less formal]
There's no way (that)

1. Yes, . . .

2. No, . . .

3. No, . . .

4. Yes, . . .

5. No, . . .

Be certain about something!

Listening: *Conclusions*

Listen and choose the best conclusion.

1. a. They think the flight isn't going to be
        on time.
    b. They think there's no chance the flight will
        be on time.
    c. They think the flight will definitely be
        on time.

2. a. Liz doesn't want to quit her job.
    b. Liz is wondering whether or not to leave
        her job.
    c. Liz definitely wants to leave her job.

3. a. Harry isn't positive he wants an instamatic.
    b. Harry is sure he wants a 35-millimeter
        camera.
    c. Harry wants an instamatic camera.

4. a. Bob was sure the market would go up.
    b. Bob admitted he was lucky.
    c. Bob doubted that the market would go up.

5. a. Shirley thinks the boss is going to give
        bonuses to everyone.
    b. Shirley is sure the boss isn't going to give
        everyone a raise.
    c. Shirley thinks there's a chance the boss is
        going to give everyone a raise.

6. a. Joe is positive there's enough soda in the
        refrigerator for the party.
    b. Joe isn't sure there's enough soda in the
        refrigerator for the party.
    c. Joe thinks there's a possibility they may
        run out of soda at the party.

Grammar Check: *Short Answers*

	A	B
1.	Are you sure you're going to be okay driving alone for five hours?	a. Yes, I do. b. Yes, I am. c. Yes, I am going.
2.	Is Celia definitely planning to get her business degree?	a. Yes, she does. b. Yes, she will. c. Yes, she is.
3.	Did Michael really say he wants to travel around the world with you?	a. No, he won't. b. No, he didn't. c. No, he doesn't.
4.	Is there any way I can help?	a. No, I don't. b. No, there isn't. c. No, you aren't.

InterChange

Look into your crystal ball and make a list of ten predictions about the
future. Share your list with the class and have other students react to it.

What are you going to do next year?

go to *law school*

(1) I'll probably
I'll most likely
I'm pretty sure I'll
Chances are I'll

(2) I'm not absolutely
positive/certain/sure.
I'm not a hundred
percent sure.

(3) in all likelihood
in all probability

A. What are you going to do next year?
B. **I'll probably**(1) go to *law school*.
A. Law school? Oh. Is that definite?
B. Well, **I'm not absolutely positive.**(2) But **in all likelihood**(3) that's what I'm going to do next year.

Where are you going to go on your vacation?

1. go on *a tour of the English countryside*

What are you going to name your new baby?

2. *Seymour*

When are you going to announce your retirement?

3. *at the next Board of Trustees meeting*

How are going to celebrate your sixteenth birthday?

How are you

4. have *a "sweet sixteen" party*

What are you going to do with your prize money?

5. buy *a yacht*

Tell somebody what you'll probably do.

98

yat
A private boat with rooms and a shop's cre

any minute now
according to the schedule

(1) It should
It ought to
It'll probably
It'll most likely
In all likelihood it'll
In all probability it'll
Chances are it'll

A. When will the next bus from Boston arrive?
B. **It should**(1) arrive any minute now.
A. Any minute now?
B. Yes, according to the schedule.

1. in half an hour
according to the recipe on
the box

2. within thirty days
according to company policy

3. in four days
according to my doctor

4. seven business days
according to usual bank
procedures

5. Minneapolis
according to the flight plan

Ask when something will happen.

	A	**B**
1.	Where is Wendy going to take ballet lessons this year?	Oh, we'll _____ send her to classes at the local elementary school. a. pretty sure b. by chance ⓒ most likely
2.	How do you think you did on your final exam?	_____ I got a B. a. In all likelihood b. In most probability c. Absolutely
3.	How many reporters will be at the press conference?	There will _____ be at least one hundred reporters there. a. more likely b. certain c. probably
4.	Who will run today's meeting?	_____ Ms. Winters will lead it. a. Chances are that b. I'm certain about that c. In probably
5.	What are you going to do with your inheritance?	I'll _____ buy some treasury bills. a. no question b. probably c. most like to
6.	Have you heard of the photographer Eliot Porter?	I'm not _____, but I think so. a. a hundred percent sure b. surely c. questioning that

InterChange

I'll probably . . .

Chances are I'll . . .

I'm pretty sure I'll . . .

Talk with a partner about future plans.

What do you think you'll be doing this weekend? next month? next summer? next winter? next year? five years from now?

Report back to the class and see if anyone has any particularly interesting or exciting plans for the future.

Listening: *What's the Meaning?*

Listen and choose the answer that is closest in meaning to the sentence you have heard.

1. a. I'm positively getting a job in a factory this summer.
    b. I'll most likely get a job in a factory this summer.
    c. In all probability he'll get a job in a factory this summer.

2. a. Our candidate will most likely win the election.
    b. There's no question that our candidate will win the election.
    c. I'm pretty sure our candidate will win the election.

3. a. The doctor is absolutely positive that Mike will recover in a few days.
    b. The doctor isn't a hundred percent sure that Mike will be okay in a few days.
    c. Mike will most likely be fine in a few days, according to the doctor.

4. a. Alice can definitely be at the meeting.
    b. Alice is positive she can make something for the meeting.
    c. Alice probably can't come to the meeting.

5. a. In all probability this paint is the right color.
    b. I'm positive this paint is the right color.
    c. I'm not certain that this paint is the right color.

6. a. Tom will probably apply to every school he has a chance of getting into.
    b. Tom will take a chance on the schools he is applying to.
    c. In all likelihood Tom will be admitted to every school he applied to.

Listening: *Where Are They?*

Listen and decide where each conversation is taking place.

1. a. in a train station
    b. in an airport
    c. in New York

2. a. in a post office
    b. in a bank
    c. in an advertising agency

3. a. in a U.S. department store
    b. in a post office in the United States
    c. in a clock shop in Germany

4. a. in a kitchen
    b. in a classroom
    c. in a dress shop

5. a. in a police station
    b. in a movie theater
    c. in a travel agency

6. a. at a presidential election convention
    b. at a racetrack
    c. at a marathon

7. a. in a toy store
    b. at the town dump
    c. in an attic

8. a. in a bank
    b. in someone's home
    c. in a hotel

9. a. in a supermarket
    b. in a theater
    c. in a restaurant

InterCultural Connections

The girl in Situation 4 on page 98 is going to celebrate her sixteenth birthday by having a *sweet sixteen* party. Traditional family celebrations include birthdays, wedding anniversaries, *wedding showers* (parties for women about to be married), and *baby showers* (parties for expectant mothers).

Tell about family occasions that are celebrated in YOUR country.

our English teacher

(1) worried
concerned
anxious
nervous

(2) I wouldn't be concerned.
I wouldn't worry.
Don't worry.
Don't be concerned.

(3) might have
may have

(4) Don't jump to conclusions.
Don't get (yourself) all
worked up.
Don't get carried away.
Don't let your imagination
run away with you.

A. You know . . . I'm getting a little **worried**(1) about our English teacher. She should have shown up for class by now.
B. **I wouldn't be concerned.**(2) She must have gotten stuck in traffic.
A. I don't know. She **might have**(3) . . . but then again, I'm not so sure. I'm afraid something must have happened.
B. Oh, come on now. **Don't jump to conclusions.**(4) I'm positive she'll show up for class soon.

1. my wife's plane

2. my husband

3. my daughter

4. our shipment of imported Christmas ornaments

5. my request for a transfer

Vocabulary Check: *What's the Expression?*

1.
Why _____ so late? We needed you an hour ago.
   a. *were you approved*
   b. *get all worked up*
   c. *did you show up* (circled)

2. Now, don't _____. I'm sure Tommy wasn't badly hurt.
   a. get tied up
   b. jump to conclusions
   c. get caught up in a lot of red tape

3. The flight _____ for Tokyo.
   a. was anxious
   b. lost track of time
   c. was late taking off

4. Captain Amory's ship has been _____ about two hours.
   a. transferred
   b. carried away
   c. delayed

5. My check finally _____ five days after I deposited it.
   a. cleared
   b. tied up
   c. proceeded

6. The _____ let the guests in to the party.
   a. policy
   b. overseas operation
   c. butler

7. Ronald's proposal _____ before it was put into effect.
   a. got caught up in a lot of red tape
   b. got all worked up
   c. was concerned

8.

I'm sorry, but I _____ in traffic!
   a. *got carried away*
   b. *got stuck*
   c. *let my imagination run away with me*

Grammar Check: *Perfect Modals*

1. I'm getting a little nervous. My mother-in-law (must   could   (should)) have been here by now.

2. I wouldn't worry. She (ought to   could   should) have gotten lost.

3. But she (might   would   should) have had an accident!

4. No. I'm sure nothing (could   might   should) have happened to her.

5. I forgot to lock the door when I left, but when I got home it was locked.
   Someone (must   should   might) have locked it for me.

6. I don't understand what went wrong. I (might   should   may) have done better on my history exam. I was really prepared for it.

7. Do you think I (should   must   may) have left my umbrella at your house? I can't find it.

8. I'm not sure why the train was late. It (might   should   ought to) have been delayed because of the stormy weather.

9. I left my car windows open and now the front seat is soaking wet! It (should   ought to   must) have rained last night.

10. Herbert was a wonderful person! Maybe I (must   should   might) have married him instead of Howard.

Which washing machine are you interested in purchasing?

buy the cheap one
buy the deluxe model

(1)	might may
(2)	On the other hand, Then again,
(3)	perhaps I'll maybe I'll I might I may
(4)	Take my advice! Take it from me! If you want my advice . . .
(5)	be disappointed be sorry regret it
(6)	I'll probably I guess I'll I suppose I'll

A. Which washing machine are you interested in purchasing?
B. I'm not sure. I **might**(1) buy the cheap one. **On the other hand**,(2) **perhaps I'll**(3) buy the deluxe model.
A. **Take my advice!**(4) Don't buy the cheap one! You'll **be disappointed**.(5)
B. Oh. Well, in that case, **I'll probably**(6) buy the deluxe model.
A. You won't be sorry.

Which movie are you going to see?

1. see *Moon Over Manhattan*
see *Dancers in Love*

How do you plan to see our beautiful city?

2. take a bus tour
walk around on my own

What kind of car are you going to request?

3. request a sub-compact
ask for a sedan

What are you going to take for your science requirement?

4. take Astronomy
take Zoology

What are you going to order?

5. order the "Chicken Surprise"
order the "Beef Delight"

You're undecided about what to do.

Vocabulary Check: *What's the Expression?*

1. _____ Don't be late for your job interview!
   a. Take my advice from me!
   b. If you want it from me!
   c. Take it from me! ⓒ

2. I'm not sure what kind of computer to buy for the office. I _____ buy an IBM or a Macintosh.
   a. maybe will
   b. might
   c. will be sorry

3. I may sell my car soon. _____, I may keep it a little longer.
   a. Take it from me
   b. I suppose
   c. On the other hand

4. Well, since you don't recommend the chicken, I'll _____ order the fish.
   a. probably
   b. perhaps will
   c. guess I'll

5. You'll be _____ if you buy those skis here. They aren't very good quality.
   a. regret
   b. sorry
   c. disappointment

6. I can't decide where to go for my vacation. France is so beautiful. _____, Greece is much warmer now.
   a. I guess
   b. Then again
   c. Probably

7. Buy that leather wallet. You won't _____.
   a. take my advice
   b. want my advice
   c. regret it

8. I _____ I'll take the rest of the day off, since I don't have any more appointments!
   a. guess
   b. am sorry
   c. supposed

InterChange

How Do You Plan to See Our Beautiful City?

The woman in Situation 2 on page 104 is a tourist and is telling her plans for seeing the city. Imagine that you are a tourist in YOUR *beautiful city or town*. Tell what you might do on a five-day visit there.

On the first day I might . . .
On the second day perhaps I'll . . .
On the third day I may . . .
On the fourth day maybe I'll . . .
And on the fifth day . . .

Have others in the class react to your plans. Perhaps they'll agree with your ideas. On the other hand, perhaps they'll have better ideas!

quit my job

(1) thinking of
considering
toying with the idea of

(2) It's a possibility.
There's a chance.
I might.
I may.
It could happen.
You never know!

A. You know . . . I'm **thinking of**(1) quitting my job.
B. Quitting your job?!
A. Yes.
B. Gee! I can't believe it! You wouldn't REALLY quit your job, would you?
A. **It's a possibility.**(2)

drop out of college

1.

go into business for myself

2.

enlist in the Navy

3.

dye my hair blonde

4.

run away from home and join the circus

5.

You're thinking of doing something drastic!

The stages in the development of children have been carefully studied and documented by noted educators and psychologists, such as Bruner, Piaget, and Spock. For a long time, it was taken for granted that once a person passed from adolescence to adulthood, few personality changes would take place. But recent studies in adult psychology have revealed that grown-ups also go through stages that are worth noting and being prepared for so that they do not come as a surprise.

Some researchers echo the wisdom of folklore and admit that different life stages last for about seven years. Others, such as Gail Sheehy in her book *Passages*, divide adult life into broader ten-year spans. Thus, there are recognizable differences in situations, problems, and solutions that women and men face when they are in their twenties, thirties, forties, and fifties.

The twenties are characterized by young people who have just passed through the dependence–independence crisis of adolescence and are striking out on their own by going away to college, joining the military, starting work, or getting married. Each of these choices brings with it different responsibilities, but in general it is a time of idealism, in which a great deal of effort is put into *getting ahead* and *proving oneself.*

The thirties bring with them a reexamination of one's original goals: a redefinition of them or a complete change. For example, a person who has been involved in academia may compete for a higher position or become disillusioned with the system and opt for a career in another area. A person who has been working his or her way up in a company may suddenly feel that the position is boring and routine and may look for a better position elsewhere or transfer to a related field. A person who has been married for several years may reassess the marriage and possibly feel that he or she has *outgrown* it. A single person may begin to look in earnest for a suitable partner. A woman who has stayed home to raise children may feel the need to return to school or work. One who has dedicated herself to a career may feel the urge to start a family.

The forties, the traditional mid-life crisis period, may bring a vague feeling of dissatisfaction with one's life and a longing for something fresh, exciting, and different. Spouse, children, and job all weigh heavily on a person who may feel that old age is approaching and may wish that life could begin again. This can be a productive time, however, because once this dilemma is resolved, there is a great sense of freedom and an accompanying desire to leave one's mark in the world while there is still time.

The fifties can usher in either bitterness and defeat, if the previous crises were not resolved, or resignation and relaxation, if they were. A person can either accept circumstances that are no longer under any control or continue to work out life's inevitable problems with perseverance and faith.

How we grow into the next passage depends on how we work out the problems of the previous one. This depends upon our knowledge of the changes adult life brings and our readiness to accept and integrate them into our daily existence.

In Your Own Words

You are the writer of a newspaper column called "Dear Emmy" in which you answer letters people send you asking for advice. Answer this reader's letter.

Dear Emmy,

I'm depressed. Yesterday was my birthday, and I'm feeling very old. All my friends are getting older. My parents are getting older, and my job isn't interesting any more. What should I do?

"Over the Hill" in Ohio

Now write your own "Dear Emmy" letter and exchange it with another student's. Answer each other's letters and then discuss your advice with the class.

(1) What do you think the chances are of
What's the likelihood of
What's the possibility of

(2) Probably not very good.
That isn't very likely.
It isn't very likely.
Pretty slim.

(3) There's not much chance of that happening.
I don't think that will happen.
I doubt (if) that will happen.

(4) In fact,
To tell the truth,

A. **What do you think the chances are of**(1) my having twins?
B. **Probably not very good.**(2) **There's not much chance of that happening.**(3)
A. Are you absolutely sure about that?
B. Yes, I'm pretty certain. **In fact,**(4) if you had twins, I'd be very surprised.

1.
2.
3.

Tell somebody there isn't much chance of something happening.

4.
5.

Function Check: *What's the Expression?*

1. What do you think the ____ are of my winning the lottery?
   a. happenings
   b. likelihoods
   c. chances *(circled)*

2. The odds are probably not ____ that our soccer team will beat the Lions.
   a. very good
   b. likely
   c. pretty slim

3. ____, if you discovered a cure for the common cold, I'd be amazed!
   a. In the fact
   b. To tell the fact
   c. To tell the truth

4. I'd probably say ____ think twice about that idea.
   a. you should
   b. you might consider to
   c. you never

5. ____ if I will be selected as an exchange student for my school.
   a. There's not much chance
   b. There's a chance
   c. I doubt

6. I don't think ____.
   a. that will happen
   b. of that to happen
   c. that much of a chance

7.

   ____. I could win the "Mr. Muscles" contest after all!
   a. I would
   b. You never think
   c. It's a possibility

Listening: *Conclusions*

Listen and choose the best conclusion.

1. a. They can definitely afford the apartment.
   b. They can probably afford the apartment. *(circled)*
   c. They definitely can't afford the apartment.

2. a. They probably will have good weather.
   b. They probably won't have good weather.
   c. They definitely won't have good weather.

3. a. He'll probably end up in Austria.
   b. He'll definitely end up in Austria.
   c. It's possible he'll end up in Austria.

4. a. It's possible that they need milk.
   b. They probably need milk.
   c. He's sure that they need milk.

5. a. Bill is definitely good enough to be on the squash team.
   b. Bill is probably not good enough to be on the squash team.
   c. Coach Johnson isn't absolutely sure Bill is good enough to be on the squash team.

6. a. They can definitely hire someone to help with the typing overload.
   b. It's possible they can hire someone to help with the typing overload.
   c. They definitely can't hire anyone to help with the typing overload.

InterView

Make up five *probability* questions about things that interest you. Take a survey of students in the class and report the results.

What do you think the chances are of . . . ?

Two friends are talking about future plans. Practice this scene with a partner.

A. I've been meaning to ask you . . .
What are you going to do when our
English course is finished?

B. I don't know. I think I might enroll in
a more advanced class.

A. Is there a good chance of your doing
that?

B. Perhaps, but I don't know for sure. If
I don't enroll in a more advanced
class, maybe I'll get a private tutor.
What do you think?

A. Excuse me?

B. What do you think I should do? Do
you have any advice?

A. Hmm. Well, I don't know. I suppose if
I had to choose between enrolling in a
more advanced class and getting a private
tutor, I'd probably enroll in a more advanced
class. But of course that's only my opinion.

B. That's interesting. Why would you do that?

A. Well, because there's an advantage to studying in
a group and being able to practice speaking with
lots of other students.

B. Hmm. That makes a lot of sense. And how about
you? What are YOU going to do when our English
course is finished?

A. . . . .

A. I've been meaning to ask you . . . What are you going to do _____?

B. I don't know. I think I might _____.

A. Is there a good chance of your doing that?

B. Perhaps, but I don't know for sure. If I don't _____, maybe I'll
_____. What do you think?

A. Excuse me?

B. What do you think I should do? Do you have any advice?

A. Hmm. Well, I don't know. I suppose if I had to choose between _____ing
and _____ing, I'd probably _____. But of course that's
only my opinion.

B. That's interesting. Why would you do that?

A. Well, because _____.

B. Hmm. That makes a lot of sense. And how about you? What are YOU going to do _____?

A. . . . .

Now create an original scene with your partner. Two friends are discussing future plans about work,
school, personal matters, and so on. You can use the model above as a guide, but feel free to adapt
and expand it any way you wish.

Function Review: *Chapters 4,5,6*

Choose the appropriate line for Speaker B.

	A	**B**
1.	Robert, why don't we stay up late and try to finish cleaning up after the party?	a. It could happen. b. I'll most likely do that. (c.) I don't really feel like cleaning up now.
2.	Don't you think Martha has been working hard lately?	(a.) I don't know about that. b. There's not much chance of that happening. c. Admit it!
3.	Are you sure that Mrs. Benton fired him?	a. Take my advice! b. I'm getting a little anxious. (c.) I'm pretty certain.
4.	Harvey, have you ever thought of singing professionally?	a. No. I don't think I'm in the mood. (b.) Yes. Maybe someday I'll try it. c. Yes. It should happen any minute now.
5.	Max, can I offer you some advice?	a. Yes. I recommend that you do. (b.) Sure. What? c. I have no doubt at all.
6.	Ronald is a fantastic dancer!	(a.) You can say that again! b. I wish he could agree. c. I suppose he's right.
7.	If I don't perform well tonight, my entire career as an opera singer will be over!	a. Wouldn't you agree with that? (b.) Now don't get yourself all worked up! c. Come on. Admit it!
8.	Professor Hunter, I need your advice on whether to drop Geology this semester.	a. I hate to disagree with you. (b.) It seems to me that you should complete the course. c. I doubt if that will happen.
9.	This city needs more police protection.	(a.) My feelings exactly. b. Is that definite? c. You'll be disappointed.
10.	I hate to admit it, but I don't think we're going to raise enough money for the new playground.	a. Positively! b. Wouldn't you agree? (c.) I'm afraid you're right.

HoMe work

Here are the expressions you practiced in Chapter 6. Try to use as many as you can to expand your vocabulary and to add variety to your use of English.

Probability/Improbability

Inquiring about . . .

What do you think the chances are of _____?
What's the likelihood of _____?
What's the possibility of _____?

Is there a good chance _____?

Expressing . . .

I'll probably _____.
I'll most likely _____.
I'm pretty sure I'll _____.
Chances are I'll _____.
I guess I'll _____.
I suppose I'll _____.

In all likelihood . . .
In all probability . . .

If I had to choose between _____ and _____, I'd probably _____.

It should
It ought to
It'll probably
It'll most likely } *arrive any minute now.*
In all likelihood it'll
In all probability it'll
Chances are it'll

The chances are probably not very good.
The chances are pretty slim.
That isn't very likely.
It isn't very likely.

There's not much chance of that happening.
I don't think that will happen.
I doubt (if) that will happen.

Fear–Worry–Anxiety

I'm (getting) (a little) { worried concerned anxious nervous } about _____.

I'm afraid something must have happened (to him/her/them).

I wouldn't be concerned.
I wouldn't worry.
Don't worry.
Don't be concerned.

Initiating a Topic

I've been meaning to ask you . . .

Focusing Attention

In fact, . . .
To tell the truth, . . .

Possibility/Impossibility

Inquiring about . . .

What's the possibility of _____?

Expressing Possibility

I might _____.
I may _____.
Perhaps I'll _____.
Maybe I'll _____.

Perhaps.

It's a possibility.
There's a chance.
I might.
I may.
It could happen.
You never know!

_____ might have _____ed.
_____ may have _____ed.

Expressing Impossibility

There's no chance (that) _____.
There's no possibility (that) _____.

[less formal]
There's no way (that) _____.

Certainty/Uncertainty

Inquiring about . . .

Are you certain/sure/positive?

Are you (absolutely) sure about that?

Is that definite?

Expressing . . .

I'm positive/certain/sure.
I'm absolutely positive/certain/sure.
Absolutely!
Positively!

I definitely _____.
There's no question (in my mind) I _____.
I have no doubt (at all) that I_____.

I'm pretty certain.

I'm not absolutely positive/certain/sure.
I'm not a hundred percent sure.
I'm not (so) sure.
I don't know for sure.

Hesitating

Hmm.
Well, . . .
Well, I don't know . . .

Persuading-Insisting

Oh, come on now.

Advice–Suggestions

Asking for . . .

What do you think (I should do)?
Do you have any advice?

Offering . . .

Take my advice!
Take it from me!
If you want my advice . . .

There's an advantage to _____ing.

Deduction

_____ must have _____.
_____ may have _____.
_____ probably _____.
_____ most likely _____.
I wouldn't be surprised if _____.
I bet _____.
Chances are _____.

Intention

Inquiring about . . .

What are you going to do (*next year*)?

You aren't really going to _____, are you?

Expressing . . .

I'm { thinking of _____ing. considering _____ing. toying with the idea of _____ing. }

Surprise–Disbelief

Quitting your job?!

Gee! I can't believe it!

You wouldn't REALLY _____, would you?

Checking and Indicating Understanding

Checking One's Own Understanding

Any minute now?

These scenes review the functions and conversation strategies in Chapters, 4, 5, and 6. Who do you think these people are? What do you think they're talking about? With other students, improvise conversations based on these scenes and act them out.

1.

2.

3.

4.

5.

6.

7.

8.

7

APPROVAL AND DISAPPROVAL
APOLOGIZING AND FORGIVING

Diane is tasting the food Roy has prepared. Do you think she likes it? What do you think they're saying to each other?

Todd is late for class. He's apologizing to his teacher and giving an explanation. What do you think he's saying to his teacher, and how do you think she's responding?

give that presentation

A. **Good job!**(1)
B. Do you really think so?
A. Yes. **Absolutely!**(2) You gave that presentation **very**(3) well.
B. I'm glad you approve.
A. As a matter of fact, I don't think I've ever seen a presentation given better than that.
B. **Thank you for saying so.**(4)

1. do that dance number

2. teach that lesson

3. run that race

4. handle that press conference

5. perform that triple-bypass operation

Express your approval of something that somebody did.

Function Check: *What's the Expression?*

1. ____, Jennifer! That was a great book report!
   a. Very well
   b. Extremely
   c. Excellent ⟵ *(circled)*

2. Thank you for ____.
   a. saying so
   b. complimenting
   c. being so nice to say

3. You played that piece ____ well, Henry.
   a. extremely
   b. exceptional
   c. unbelievable

4. It's ____ of you to say that.
   a. unbelievable
   b. compliment
   c. nice

5. You performed your gymnastics routine ____, Tanya.
   a. positively
   b. very good
   c. extremely well

6. Thank you for the ____.
   a. saying
   b. compliment
   c. niceness

Listening: *Where Are They?*

Listen and decide where each conversation is taking place.

1. a. in a supermarket
   b. in someone's home ⟵ *(circled)*
   c. in a bakery

2. a. in a card shop
   b. in a car assembly plant
   c. in an auto repair shop

3. a. in a cab
   b. in someone's home
   c. in a laboratory

4. a. in a paint store
   b. in a museum
   c. in a hardware store

5. a. in a classroom
   b. in someone's home
   c. in a reception area of an office

6. a. in a barber shop
   b. at a customer service desk
   c. in an airport

On Stage!

Perform something for the class—sing a song, do a little dance, recite a poem, hum, whistle . . . anything you wish! The other students will respond enthusiastically and compliment you on your performance.

117

clip Fifi's hair

A. **Do you approve of the way I**[1] clipped Fifi's hair?
B. Well . . . Can I **be frank**[2] with you?
A. **By all means.**[3] Please.
B. **In all honesty,**[4] I think Fifi's hair could have been clipped a little better.
A. Come to think of it, you're probably right. **Please accept my apology.**[5] I promise I'll do better next time.

[1] Do you approve of the way I ____ed?
How do you like the way I ____ed?
What do you think of the way I ____ed?
What do you think of how I ____ed?
Did I ____ all right?

[2] be frank
be honest
be open
level

[3] By all means.
Sure.
Yes.

[4] In all honesty,
To be (perfectly) honest,
To be (perfectly) frank,

[5] Please accept my apology.
Please forgive me.
I apologize.
I'm sorry.

1. type the report

2. assemble this radio

3. handle the union negotiations

4. prepare the spaghetti sauce

5. fly the plane

Ask for somebody else's approval of something you did.

Grammar Check: *Passive Modals*

	A	**B**
1.	How do you like the way I rearranged our office?	Well, to be frank, I think I ____ before you changed everything. a. must have been consulted (b.) should have been consulted c. would have been consulted
2.	Did I put enough sugar in the iced tea?	Sure. It ____ any sweeter. a. shouldn't be made b. wouldn't have been made c. can't have been made
3.	I'm really concerned. The surgeons have been in the operating room for more than five hours.	Don't you think we ____ by now if something had gone wrong? a. must have been told b. would have been told c. could have been told
4.	I'm sorry I mishandled the Acme account. I promise I'll do better next time.	If you want to keep your job, it ____ better next time! a. must be handled b. would be handled c. could be handled
5.	I hope your son likes chocolate frosting, Mrs. Murphy.	Oh, no! The cake ____ with vanilla frosting! a. could have been iced b. would have been iced c. should have been iced
6.	Please accept my apology for breaking one of your favorite glasses.	Well, I suppose it might have been worse. All my glasses ____! a. should have been broken b. could have been broken c. must have been broken

InterChange

Asking for Feedback

The people on page 118 are all *asking for feedback*. They want to know how well they have done their job. Do you think it's important for people to ask for feedback? Why or why not? How about you? Do you ask for feedback? How do you react to it?

raise your voice to the boss

(1) it's none of my business
I'm out of place saying so
it isn't my place to say so
I'm speaking out of turn

[less formal]
I'm sticking my nose
    where it doesn't' belong

(2) what(ever) prompted you
        to do it
what(ever) got into you
what(ever) possessed you

(3) I suppose you're right.
I guess you're right.
You're probably right.

A. You know . . . perhaps **it's none of my business**(1), but you really shouldn't have raised your voice to the boss.
B. Oh?
A. Yes. I don't know **whatever prompted you to do it**,(2) but it probably wasn't a good idea.
B. Hmm. **I suppose you're right.**(3)

1. take yesterday off without permission

2. invite your entire sixth-grade class to your birthday party

3. contradict the principal at today's faculty meeting

4. disregard the warning light on the dashboard

5. tell the bank teller your real name

You think somebody shouldn't have done something.

120

remove the coffee machine

A. You know . . . I hate to say it, but I really wish you hadn't removed the coffee machine.
B. Oh? Why?
A. Employee morale is at an all-time low!
B. **I apologize.**(1) If I had **known**(4) that employee morale was going to be at an all-time low, I wouldn't have removed it.

(1) I apologize.
I'm sorry.
Please forgive me.

[more formal]
Please accept my apology.

(2) known
realized

1. let Peter have the car tonight

2. ask for garlic and pepperoni on this pizza

3. promise the kids new bicycles for Christmas

4. make me get such a short haircut

5. tell the foreman how fast we can produce these teddy bears

You wish somebody hadn't done something.

Listening: *What's the Meaning?*

Listen and choose the answer that is closest in meaning to the sentence you have heard.

1. a. I know it isn't my business, but I don't think you should talk behind the teacher's back.
   b. Perhaps it's not my business, but you really shouldn't talk to the teacher.
   c. Maybe I'm out of place saying so, but you shouldn't argue with the teacher.

2. a. Were you responsible for Bill's changing from being a Republican to a Democrat?
   b. Bill, what possessed you to switch from being a Republican to being a Democrat?
   c. Bill, you were very prompt to change from being a Republican to being a Democrat.

3. a. I know this isn't my place, but I could sue you for the work you did.
   b. I know I'm speaking out of turn, but you could lose your suit.
   c. Perhaps it's none of my business, but you need a new suit for work.

4. a. I don't know why you decided to write to the president of the phone company.
   b. I don't know what impressed you about the letter from the president of the phone company.
   c. I don't know what depressed you about the letter from the president of the phone company.

5. a. I suggest that you not spend your time on video games.
   b. I guess I might have spent my last quarter on that video game.
   c. You're probably right. I shouldn't have used my last quarter on that video game.

Function Check: *What's My Line?*

Choose the appropriate line for Speaker B.

	A	**B**
1.	Do you approve of the way I organized the political rally?	a. Whatever possessed you? b. I supposed you're right. c. In all honesty, it could have been better organized.
2.	You know . . . perhaps it's none of my business, but you shouldn't have driven through that stop sign.	a. If I had realized it was there, I would have stopped. b. If I hadn't realized it was there, I would have stopped. c. I hadn't thought I realized it was there.
3.	Didn't you realize that as a result of your withdrawing $200 from our account, we can't write any more checks until I get paid?	a. It's none of my business. b. Whatever possessed you? c. Please forgive me.
4.	Can I be frank with you?	a. I'm sorry. b. By all means. c. If I had only known.
5.	How do you like the way I carved the Thanksgiving turkey?	a. You're probably right. b. Please accept my apology. c. Well, to be honest, I think you could have done a better job.

When people offer each other constructive criticism (that is, criticism that is intended to be helpful), they usually preface the critical comments with apologetic remarks so that the person criticized is not offended. The tone of voice, usually hesitant and sincere, combined with appropriate facial expressions and gestures, conveys the fact that the remarks are meant to help rather than hurt. The person being criticized may respond by indicating surprise, lack of awareness, or an admission that the criticism is deserved.

Criticism can be offered in other ways. Teasing a person or joking about an issue is a common way of expressing constructive criticism. The person being criticized may ignore, laugh off, or acknowledge the criticism, but both parties know that the message has been delivered and received.

An indirect way of expressing criticism is to involve a third person. Asking someone who is very close to the person being criticized to speak on your behalf is a thoughtful act. Although it is difficult to accept criticism under any circumstances, being confronted by a good friend can make a difficult situation less so.

Sometimes people soften criticism by prefacing their remarks with an acknowledgment of the good qualities of the person being criticized or by a statement of appreciation of the strength of a friendship or a relationship. Typical remarks used to preface criticism are "I think you're doing an excellent job here, but there are one or two little things you may want to keep in mind" and "We're good friends, aren't we? May I level with you about something?"

Knowing how to give constructive criticism in a variety of ways and knowing how to take criticism with the proper attitude are essential parts of effective communication between people at home, at work or school, and in the community at large.

InterAct!

With a partner, choose one of the following situations and create a scene in which one person gives the other *constructive criticism*. Then present your scenes to the class and ask for THEIR *constructive criticism*!

Dorothy and Dan are in the same calculus class. Dorothy is very good in math. She always figures out all the problems before the other students, and she often calls out the answers in class before others have finished their work. Everybody in the class is annoyed when she does this. Dan has decided to call this to her attention.

Robert is the sales manager of a successful company. Lately he has been cold and aloof in the office and hasn't responded to people's greetings. Several employees have spoken to Angela, the personnel director of the company. Angela has decided to invite Robert to lunch in an effort to bring up this sensitive subject with him.

be late

(1) I apologize for
Forgive me for

[less formal]
Sorry for

(2) That's okay.
It's okay.
That's all right.
It's all right.

(3) I'm really sorry.
I'm very sorry.
I feel terrible.

(4) Don't worry about it.
No problem.

A. **I apologize for**[1] being late.
B. **That's okay.**[2]
A. You know, this is the first time I've ever been late. **I'm really sorry.**[3]
B. **Don't worry about it.**[4]

1. forget our anniversary

2. fall asleep in class

3. shout at you

4. come back late from lunch

5. mess up my lines

Apologize to somebody.

(1) I'd like to apologize
I want to apologize
I've got to apologize

(2) I'm really sorry about it.
I really regret it.

(3) I hope you'll forgive me.
Please forgive me.

(4) These things happen.
We all make mistakes.
You're only human.

A. **I'd like to apologize**(1) for behaving rudely at your party last night.
B. It's all right.
A. **I'm really sorry about it.**(2) **I hope you'll forgive me.**(3)
B. Don't worry about it. **These things happen.**(4)

1.
2.
3.
4.
5.

Listening: *Who Are They?*

Listen and decide what the relationship between the two speakers is.

1. a. clerk–store owner
   b. lifeguard–pool director
   c. housekeeper–homeowner

2. a. husband–wife
   b. boss–secretary
   c. teacher–student

3. a. sergeant–private
   b. cook–waiter
   c. father–child

4. a. student–teacher
   b. doctor–patient
   c. roommate–roommate

5. a. police officer–driver
   b. guest–host
   c. lawyer–criminal

6. a. butcher–customer
   b. tailor–customer
   c. hairdresser–customer

Listening: *What's the Meaning?*

Listen and choose the answer that is closest in meaning to the sentence you have heard.

1. a. I'm sorry I didn't go to Spain while you were there.
   b. I'm sorry I never apologized for not writing to you in Spain.
   c. I'm sorry I didn't write to you in Spain while you were there.

2. a. I apologize for burning the chicken.
   b. Please forgive me for burning the kitchen.
   c. Please don't give me the burnt chicken.

3. a. I feel so sick when I'm in the hospital.
   b. It's terrible being in the hospital.
   c. I'm really sorry you're in the hospital.

4. a. That's right. I'm not usually late.
   b. It's all right. I know you're usually not late.
   c. That's all right. I know you're usually late.

5. a. You'd better finish the exam in a hurry.
   b. Don't worry about finishing the exam.
   c. Don't try to finish the exam.

6. a. That's okay. There's still some water left.
   b. Don't worry. I still haven't ordered.
   c. It's okay. You only spilled water.

Grammar Check: *Gerunds and Infinitives*

1. Tim apologized for (to leave (leaving)) his younger sister home alone.

2. Shirley said she wanted (to travel, traveling) for a while before she went to college.

3. Ed hopes (to become becoming) a successful jazz musician in a few years.

4. I'm sorry. My secretary failed (to inform informing) you that I had to cancel our appointment.

5. Congratulations! We've decided (to award awarding) you the medal for outstanding oratory skills.

6. Bob and I regret (to have having) to go so early, but the baby-sitter has to be home by 10:00.

7. Oh, no! It's 11:30, and I forgot (to go going) to the airport to pick up my boss!

8. We considered (to move moving) back to the city, but the truth is we really enjoy (to live living) on the farm.

9. In my opinion, we need (to consider considering) other alternatives before we make our final decision.

10. I'm really sorry about not (to let letting) you know about the emergency meeting that was scheduled.

1.

Mrs. Ruggles, I'd _____ apologize for throwing my baseball through your window.
 a. want to
 b. regret to
 ⓒ like to

2. Steven, about that spot on your new tie . . . I'm really _____ it.
 a. sorry for
 b. regret
 c. sorry about

3. Donald, I've _____ apologize for starting a rumor about you. It was a joke.
 a. got to
 b. hoped to
 c. liked to

4. You can stop worrying about the dish you broke. These things _____.
 a. are all mistakes
 b. are regrettable
 c. happen

5. Don't worry about the stain on the rug, Joan. We all _____.
 a. make these things happen
 b. make mistakes
 c. make human mistakes

6.

_____ forgive me for forgetting your last name, Wally.
 a. I hope to
 b. Please
 c. You'll only

InterChange

Fill in the following with names of students in the class.

You smashed into _Vic_'s car!

You lost all of _Tiffty_'s books you had borrowed!

You accidentally stepped on ~~Ezra~~ Travis's foot!

You laughed during _Sam_'s speech the other day.

You forgot to call _Abdlou_ back last weekend.

You interrupted _Mr. Thompson_ when he or she was just talking.

You gave _Norker_ the wrong information about yesterday's homework assignment!

You . . . .

Now apologize to those students, and they will (hopefully) forgive you.

Your hamburgers are overcooked.

Dad

(1) upset
annoyed
taken aback

(2) Maybe you ought to _____.
Maybe you should _____.
Maybe you should consider _____ing.
It might be a good idea to _____.
Why don't you _____?

(3) patch things up
clear the air
smooth things over
iron things out
set things straight

A. You know, I think you hurt Dad's feelings when you told him his hamburgers were overcooked.
B. Hmm. I didn't realize that. Do you think he's angry with me?
A. I don't know if "angry" is the right word, but it seems to me he's a little **upset**.(1)
B. Gee. I feel terrible.
A. **Maybe you ought to**(2) apologize to him. That might help **patch things up**(3) between the two of you.
B. Good idea! I'll do that.

You're a little overweight.

1. Michael

You're spoiling your grandchildren.

2. your mother

Your new jingle for Sudsy Soap isn't creative enough.

3. Barry

We're spending too much time on grammar, and not enough on conversation.

4. our English teacher

Your new boyfriend is a "nerd."

5. your sister

You hurt somebody's feelings. Maybe you ought to apologize.

128

Vocabulary Check: *What's the Expression?*

1.
> *Now let's stop fighting and ____ straight!*
> a. smooth things
> ⓑ set things
> c. iron things

2. Don't give the children everything they want, Harry. They'll be ____.
   a. spoiled
   b. upset
   c. "the laughing stock"

3. One of our employees ____ stealing cash from the company vault.
   a. failed
   b. occurred
   c. was accused of

4. Until we ____ with our supervisor, office relations were terrible.
   a. behaved rudely
   b. cleared the air
   c. hit an all time low

5. The steaks look like charcoal! I guess they're ____.
   a. overweight
   b. patched up
   c. overcooked

6.
> *I was so worried about my English exam that I didn't ____.*
> a. mess up
> b. sleep a wink
> c. shout

Grammar Check: *Sequence of Tenses*

Choose the statement that best reports the direct quote.

1. "You're trying too hard to impress the boss."
   a. He told me I'm trying too hard to impress the boss.
   ⓑ He told me I was trying too hard to impress the boss.
   c. He told me you're trying too hard to impress the boss.

2. "It may be a good idea to cut back on production for a while."
   a. He announced that may it be a good idea to cut back on production for a while.
   b. He announced that it might be a good idea to cut back on production for a while.
   c. He announced that it would be a good idea to cut back on production for a while.

3. "Why didn't you explain the homework to us?"
   a. The class asked me why I didn't explain the homework to them.
   b. The class asked me if I hadn't explained the homework to them.
   c. The class asked me why I hadn't explained the homework to them.

4. "Will you be mad at me if I go to the party without you?"
   a. She wondered if I am going to be mad at her if she goes to the party without me.
   b. She wondered if I will be mad at her if she went to the party without me.
   c. She wondered if I would be mad at her if she went to the party without me.

> *Maybe you ought to apologize.*
>
> *Good idea. I'll do that.*

With a partner, create scenes in which the people on page 128 apologize to the people whose feelings they hurt.

One friend is apologizing to another because he can't keep a promise. Practice this scene with a partner.

gen

A. You're going to have to forgive me.
B. Oh? Why?
A. Well, remember I had promised you I'd help you study for the TOEFL* exam?
B. Yes. I remember.
A. Well, **I hate to have to tell you this**,(1) but I'm afraid I can't keep my promise.
B. Oh? Why not?
A. Well . . . you see . . . I have to go to the Immigration Office to renew my visa. Otherwise, I'd be able to help you study for the *fa-full →* TOEFL exam.
B. That's okay. I understand.
A. You know, **I don't usually break promises.**(2) I hope you're not upset with me.
B. No, not at all. **These things happen.**(3)

(1) I hate to have to tell you this
   I don't feel very good about telling you this
   I wish I didn't have to tell you this

(2) I don't usually break promises.
   I don't make a habit of breaking promises.
   I'm not one to go back on my word.

(3) These things happen.
   It's not your fault.

A. You're going to have to forgive me.
B. Oh? Why?
A. Well, remember I had promised you I'd _____?
B. Yes, I remember.
A. Well, **I hate to have to tell you this**,(1) but I'm afraid I can't keep my promise.
B. Oh? Why not?
A. Well . . . you see . . . _____.
   Otherwise, I'd be able to _____.
B. That's okay. I understand.
A. You know, **I don't usually break promises to people.**(2) I hope you're not upset with me.
B. No, not at all. **These things happen.**(3)

Now create an original scene with your partner. One of you is apologizing to the other. You can use the model above as a guide, but feel free to adapt and expand it any way you wish.

* TOEFL: Test of English as a Foreign Language.

Function Check: *What's My Line?*

Choose the appropriate line for Speaker B.

	A	**B**
1.	What's wrong?	a. I'm not one to go back on my word. b. These things happen. ⓒ I hate to tell you this, but you have to work overtime tonight.
2.	Because of my mistake, we're going to have to run the computer program all over again!	a. I wish I didn't have to tell you this, but we have to run it again. b. Don't worry. It's not your fault. c. Maybe you should consider forgiving him.
3.	I think you ought to talk to Greg. He's very upset with you.	a. Maybe you're right. That might help clear the air. b. I don't feel very good about telling you this. c. He's taken aback.
4.	I hope your mother's not too upset with me for spilling ketchup on her new white tablecloth.	a. I don't make a habit of breaking promises to people. b. Why don't you forgive her? c. Maybe you ought to apologize to her.
5.	I hope you're not upset with me.	a. I hate to have to tell you this. b. It's not your fault. Don't worry. I understand. c. I wish I didn't have to tell you, but I'm not one to go back on my word.
6.	Why is Carl sitting by himself in the corner?	a. He's ironing things out. b. He's considering. c. He's upset.

In Your Own Words

For Writing and Discussion

Have you ever broken a promise you had made to someone?

What had you promised?
Why did you break the promise?
How did the other person react?
Did you later wish you hadn't broken it?

Here are the expressions you practiced in Chapter 7. Try to use as many as you can to expand your vocabulary and to add variety to your use of English.

Approval/Disapproval

Inquiring about . . .

Do you approve of the way I _____ed?
How do you like the way I _____ed?
What do you think of the way I _____ed?
What do you think of how I _____ed?
Did I _____ all right?

Expressing Approval

Good job!
Fine job!
Well done!
Excellent!
Very good!

Good idea!

You _____ed { very well.
extremely well.
exceptionally well.
unbelievably well. }

Expressing Disapproval

In all honesty, _____.
To be (perfectly) honest, _____.
To be (perfectly) frank, _____.

I think _____ could have been _____ed better.

You (really) shouldn't have _____ed.

I (really) wish you hadn't _____ed.

As a result of your _____ing, _____.

Initiating a Topic

Perhaps it's none of my business, but...
Perhaps I'm out of place saying so, but...
Perhaps it isn't my place to say so, but...
Perhaps I'm speaking out of turn, but...

[less formal]
Perhaps I'm sticking my nose where it doesn't belong, but . . .

You know, . . .

I hate to say it . . . but . . .

Complimenting

Expressing Compliments

I don't think I've ever seen a _____ better than _____.

Apologizing

I apologize.
I'm sorry.
Please forgive me.

[more formal]
Please accept my apology.

I apologize
Forgive me
[less formal]
Sorry } for _____ing.

I'd like to apologize
I want to apologize
I've got to apologize } for _____ing.

I'm really sorry.
I'm really sorry about it.
I'm very sorry.
I feel terrible.
I really regret it.

I hope you'll forgive me.
Please forgive me.

You're going to have to forgive me.

Granting Forgiveness

That's okay.
It's okay.
That's all right.
It's all right.
Don't worry about it.
No problem.
These things happen.
We all make mistakes.
You're only human.
It's not your fault.
I understand.

Promising

Offering a Promise

I promise I'll _____.
I had promised (_____) I'd _____.

Breaking a Promise

I can't keep my promise.

I don't usually break promises.
I don't make a habit of breaking promises.
I'm not one to go back on my word.

Wish–Hope

I hope _____.

Remembering/Forgetting

Inquiring about . . .

Remember I had promised you I'd _____?

Indicating . . .

I remember.

Denying/Admitting

Admitting

I hate to have to tell you this, but . . .
I don't feel very good about telling you this, but . . .
I wish I didn't have to tell you this, but . . .

Gratitude

Expressing . . .

Thank you for *saying so*.
Thank you for *the compliment*.
It's nice of you to *say that*.
It's nice of you to *say so*.

Agreement/Disagreement

Expressing Agreement

I suppose you're right.
I guess you're right.
You're probably right.

Advice–Suggestions

Offering . . .

Maybe you ought to _____.
Maybe you should _____.
Maybe you should consider _____ing.
It might be a good idea to _____.
Why don't you _____?

Responding to . . .

I hadn't thought of that.
That hadn't occurred to me.
That never entered my mind.

Hesitating

Well . . .
You know . . .
Come to think of it . . .
You see . . .

8

REGRETS
WISHES

The weather is bad today. Melissa and her brother Roger wish the weather were better. What do you think they're saying to each other?

Linda's teacher, Ms. Anderson, is concerned about her. Ms. Anderson has decided to take some action. She regrets it, but she feels she doesn't have any choice. What do you think Ms. Anderson has decided, and why? What do you think they're saying to each other?

Speech bubble: *This restaurant is so **expensive**! We can't eat here tonight.*

(1) It's a shame (that)
    It's a pity (that)
    I'm disappointed (that)
    It's disappointing (that)
    It's too bad (that)

    [less formal]
    Too bad

(2) I agree (with you).
    You're right.
    That's right.
    That's true.
    I know.

(3) Me, too.
    I think so, too.
    I feel the same way.

(4) it looks like
    it seems like
    it seems as if
    it seems as though

A. **It's a shame**(1) this restaurant is so expensive.
B. **I agree.**(2) I wish it were cheaper.
A. **Me, too.**(3) I was hoping we could eat here tonight, but **it looks like**(4) that's out of the question.
B. I'm afraid so.

1. *The weather is so **bad**! We can't go to the beach.*

2. *This machine is so **slow**! We won't be able to finish copying this report today.*

3. *The boss is in such a **bad mood**! I can't ask him to give me tomorrow off.*

4. *The union's wage demands are so **high**! We won't be able to negotiate an agreement by midnight.*

5. *These instructions are so **complicated**! We won't be able to put this bicycle together for Patty's birthday.*

Express regret about something.

134

Grammar Check: *Wish Clauses*

1.

   The elevator in the building doesn't work. I wish it _____ so that I wouldn't have to carry my groceries up the stairs.
   - a. works
   - b. has worked
   - (c.) worked

2. Alfred has been with the company for three years, so he's getting a promotion. I wish I _____ a promotion.
   - a. were getting
   - b. am getting
   - c. have been getting

3. The sales representative from your company didn't come yesterday. I wish she _____ so that we could have given her our order.
   - a. had come
   - b. came
   - c. would come

4. I went all the way to Mason's Lumber Yard to buy some wood, and they were closed. I wish I _____ they were closed on Sundays.
   - a. knew
   - b. had known
   - c. would know

5. I can't go to the art exhibit tomorrow. I wish I _____, but I have to paint my house.
   - a. could have
   - b. could
   - c. can

6. It's a shame we can't supply you with the merchandise you wanted. I wish we _____ you.
   - a. could be able to help
   - b. could help
   - c. can help

7. The morale of our hockey team is really low. I wish we _____ a game soon to boost our spirits.
   - a. won
   - b. will win
   - c. would win

8.

   I didn't bring my umbrella to work and now it's raining. I wish it _____.
   - a. weren't
   - b. hadn't been
   - c. isn't

It's a shame that . . . !

It's too bad that . . . !

I'm disappointed that . . . !

It's a pity that . . . !

Take a few minutes to *get things off your chest*—express things you're feeling frustrated or disappointed about. Maybe other students in the class have some solutions or different ways of looking at things!

(1) It's too bad (that)
     It's a shame (that)
     It's a pity (that)

(2) That's exactly what I was
         thinking.
     That's exactly what I
         think.
     That's just what I was
         thinking.

     [less formal]
     You can say that again!
     You took the words right
         out of my mouth!

A. You know what I wish?
B. What?
A. I wish we had a newer car.
B. I know. **It's too bad**[1] we don't. If we had a newer car, we
    wouldn't spend so much money on repairs.
A. **That's exactly what I was thinking.**[2]

1.

2.

3.

4.

5.

Tell what you wish.

Grammar Check: *Conditionals*

1. It's too bad we don't have any film in our camera. If we ((had) have   had had) film, we could take pictures of the animals at the zoo.

2. If you had behaved, Tracy, I (had   would have   will have) bought some ice cream.

3. If I could just see her one more time, I (could have   would have   would) feel better.

4. If Jean had more sense, she (couldn't   wouldn't   didn't) go riding around on a motorcycle!

5. I wonder what Henry would do if I (threw   had thrown   would throw) a pie in his face!

Reading: *Used Cars*

People buy used cars for several reasons. One may be that they have a limited amount of money to spend. Another may be that they want a second, less expensive car for other members of the family to use. Whatever the reason, buying a used car is often a headache, both before and after the transaction. What appears to be a *cream puff* may prove to be a *lemon*!

A tedious task is locating the best used car within the price range you have in mind. This can be done by looking through the classified section of the newspaper, by going to different used-car dealers, or by keeping an eye out for FOR SALE signs in public places.

Once a car is found, it should be test-driven and examined closely or taken to a mechanic for a prepurchase inspection. Once the buyer and seller agree on a price and money changes hands, the new owner can only hope that he or she has made the right choice.

In response to many consumer complaints about unscrupulous used-car dealers, the Federal Trade Commission now requires dealers to place stickers on used cars telling whether the car is being sold *as is* or if there is a warranty. This way, buyers know who is responsible for repairs on the car in case something goes wrong after the sale. The stickers are legal contracts that spell out exactly what is covered by the warranty, if there is one.

Even this measure is no guarantee against having to pay for major repairs after a used car has been paid for. Over time, cars deteriorate. A car that appears to be in good condition today may fall apart tomorrow. More often than not, the difference between purchasing a *cream puff* or a *lemon* is a matter of luck.

InterChange

Have you ever bought a used car? Do you know anyone who has bought one? Was the car a *cream puff* or a *lemon*? Tell about it.

your new job?

I can't communicate with my boss.

(1) I've been meaning
I keep forgetting
I keep meaning

(2) Do you really want to know?
Do you want to know the truth?

(3) the truth is
the fact of the matter is

(4) That's too bad!
That's a shame!
That's a pity!
What a shame!
What a pity!

(5) If only I could
I wish I could

(6) It's not that easy.
It's not that simple.
It's easier said than done.

A. **I've been meaning**(1) to ask you. How are you enjoying your new job?
B. **Do you really want to know?**(2)
A. Yes.
B. Well, **the truth is,**(3) I'm not enjoying my new job at all.
A. Oh. **That's too bad!**(4) I'm sorry to hear that.
B. **If only I could**(5) communicate with my boss.
A. Why can't you?
B. **It's not that easy.**(6) Communicating with my boss is very difficult.
A. I'm sure it is. But don't give up trying.
B. Oh, don't worry. I won't.

college?

I can't change my major.

1.

retirement?

I can't keep busy.

2.

139

	A	**B**

1.	I've been _____ to ask you how you're enjoying being on the fencing team.
	   a. keeping
	   (b.) meaning
	   c. knowing
		It's great. I'm enjoying it a lot.

2.	If _____ I could convince the coach to let me play more, I know I could do a good job!
	   a. I wish
	   b. only
	   c. I mean
		I know what you mean.

3.	It's _____ than done.
	   a. not that easy
	   b. said
	   c. easier said
		I know, but don't give up trying.

4.	I _____ to tell you about my new drum set.
	   a. keep forgetting
	   b. always forget
	   c. mean to forget
		I didn't know you got a new drum set!

5.	I wish I _____ get used to American food. I miss my mother's cooking!
	   a. will
	   b. do
	   c. could
		I'm sure you do!

6.	What do you think about our new economic policy?	Do you really _____ what I think about it?
		   a. mean to know
		   b. wish you could know
		   c. want to know

7.	How does it feel to be new in town?	Well, the fact of _____ is, I'm a little lonely.
		   a. the truth
		   b. it
		   c. the matter

8.	My mother has been very sick lately.	That's too _____. I'm sorry to hear that.
		   a. pity
		   b. bad
		   c. shame

Listen and choose the best response.

1. a. Yes.
   b. Do you really want to know?
   c. I keep forgetting.

2. a. I only wish I could.
   b. I want to know the truth.
   c. What a shame!

3. a. That's too bad.
   b. It's easier said than done.
   c. What a pity!

4. a. It's not that comfortable.
   b. That's a shame!
   c. It's the fact of the matter.

5. a. If I could only work so hard.
   b. I keep meaning to ask you.
   c. The truth is, it's hard work.

6. a. If only I could speak to the other senators.
   b. Do you really want to know?
   c. I wish it could.

InterAct!

The people on pages 138 and 139 need your help! As a class, brainstorm effective ways for each of them to solve their problems.

- I need to learn how to communicate with my boss.
- I have to figure out a way to change my major.
- I've got to discover ways of keeping busy.
- I have to learn how to deal with my landlord.
- I've got to figure out how I can meet people.
- I need to come up with ways of keeping up with the other students.
- I wish I could figure out the New York subway system!
- How can I get used to taking orders in the army?
- Will I ever be able to memorize all those irregular English verbs?!
- There's got to be a way for me to get along better with the press and Congress!

Then, with a partner, choose one of the situations and create a second, more *positive* conversation. For example:

- Tell me, have you figured out ways to communicate with your boss?
- I sure have! Here's what I do now. I . . .

A. I wish I hadn't forgotten to fill up the tank before we left!
B. **Do you mean to say**[1] we're out of gas?!
A. Yes, and **it's all my fault!**[2] **I made a terrible mistake!**[3]

[1] Do you mean (to say) Are you saying Does that mean	[2] It's all my fault! I'm entirely to blame!	[3] I made a terrible mistake! [less formal] I (really) goofed! I (really) blew it!

1.

2.

Function Check: *What's My Line?*

	A	**B**

1.	I wish I _____ lost my license!
	   a. had
	   (b.) hadn't
	   c. didn't
		You lost your license?!

2.	I really _____ mistake. I forgot to put a stamp on the tax forms I just mailed.
	   a. blew my
	   b. goofed my
	   (c.) made a terrible
		I don't believe it!

3.	Do you mean _____ you didn't pay the telephone bill last month?
	   (a.) to say
	   b. to mean
	   c. to be saying
		I'm sorry. I completely forgot.

4.	I'm entirely _____. I forgot to set the timer, so I'm afraid the roast burned.
	   a. fault
	   b. my goof
	   (c.) to blame
	       blām^m
		Don't worry about it.

5.	I'm sorry that your goldfish died. It's all _____.
	   a. my blame
	   b. my shoulders
	   (c.) my fault
	       fault
		No, it isn't.

In Your Own Words

For Writing and Discussion

I wish I had . . .

I wish I hadn't . . .

If I had . . .

If I hadn't . . .

We all wish we had done some things differently in our lives. Tell about things you wish YOU had done differently. How do you think your life would be different if you had done those things?

Vocabulary Check: *What's the Word?*

1. I really blew it! I (passed (flunked)) my math test!

2. The company had to (lay off) wave) a lot of its best employees because it was going bankrupt.

3. Did you (negotiate (neglect) to leave your keys at the front desk?

4. It's your own (mood (fault) that you missed class. You forgot to set the alarm.

5. Our ((wages) tanks) are too low. We want a raise.

6. My uncle had a very ((complicated) irregular) operation, but luckily he's all right.

7. My mother (blew up (gave up) trying to convince me to become a violist.

8. I'm sorry. Ms. Walters won't be (convenient (available) until later in the day.

9. It's very (disappointed (disappointing) that our profits were so low this year.

10. I'm so frustrated! The used car I just bought turned out to be a real (cream puff (lemon)!

Vocabulary Check: *What's the Preposition?*

1. I don't understand why we're almost out of gas. I just had the tank filled (out   in (up)).

2. When are you ever going to give (in (up) on) eating those rich desserts?

3. Why do you keep putting (off) out   in) doing your homework?

4. My parents don't understand me. I really can't seem to communicate (to (with) from) them.

5. Do you and your older brother get (down (along   in)?

6. Mrs. Rogers, I put those computer printouts (at   on (in) your office.

7. Mr. Franklin, would you please put (on (together) off) a comprehensive report about your work? We need it for our files.

8. The president waved (in   into (to) the crowd as he boarded the plane in Geneva.

9. I'm sorry. That's completely (into (out of   along) the question!

InterChange

The people on pages 142 and 143 are in some real predicaments! What would YOU do if you were *in their shoes*?

What would you do if you ran out of gas on the highway?
What would you do if your dog ran away?
What would you do if you were lost in the woods without a compass?
What would you do if you were picked up for speeding and you had forgotten to renew your license?
What would you do if you were a zookeeper and a lion escaped from your zoo?

(1) I regret (that) I _____.
I'm sorry (that) I _____.
I regret _____ing.
I'm sorry about _____ing.

(2) choice
alternative
other option
other recourse

(3) I wasn't aware of that.
I didn't know that.

(4) Under the circumstances
Given the circumstances
Given the situation

A. You know, **I regret that I**(1) have to fire Mr. Smith.
B. Why are you going to do it?
A. I don't have any **choice.**(2) He was caught embezzling funds from the bank.
B. Oh! **I wasn't aware of that.**(3)
A. If he hadn't been caught embezzling funds from the bank, I wouldn't have to fire him.
B. **Under the circumstances,**(4) I can see why you have to do it.

1.

2.

3.

4.

5.

You regret that you have to do something.

Function Check: *What's My Line?*

	A	**B**
1.	Why are you sending your manuscript to another publisher?	I don't have any _____. The first one didn't want to publish it. a. alternator (b.) other option c. choosing
2.	Did you know that Ernest Bradley was expelled from school today?	Oh, no! I _____ that. a. regret b. wasn't aware of c. know
3.	Can I make one more phone call?	Well, _____ the circumstances, you're allowed only one call. a. under b. aware of c. sorry about
4.	Mrs. Weatherby is sixty-five, so she has to retire.	a. I wasn't given any other choice. b. Evidently, she's retiring. c. I know. She regrets having to retire.
5.	The new dishwasher you installed hasn't worked since the day you put it in.	a. I'm sorry that you've been inconvenienced. b. There isn't any other option. c. Given the situation, you didn't know that.
6.	Ben was picked up by the police for hitchhiking.	a. He didn't have any other recourse. b. Perhaps he didn't know it was illegal. c. Given the situation, he was caught.

InterCultural Connections

Many people do their shopping in large shopping malls. As a result, many smaller stores are forced to close, such as the store in Situation 6 on page 146. Does this happen in YOUR country? Tell about shopping where you're from.

People are talking about things they regret. Practice these scenes with a partner.

A. You know, I've been thinking.
B. What?
A. I regret I didn't start studying English when I was young. I wish I had begun when I was about five or so.
B. What makes you say that?
A. If I had begun studying English earlier, I wouldn't be having so much trouble with pronunciation.
B. I can understand why you feel that way.

A. You know, I've been thinking.
B. What?
A. I'm sorry I'm so shy. I wish I felt more comfortable around large groups of people.
B. What makes you say that?
A. If I weren't so shy, I wouldn't feel so uneasy at parties like these.
B. I can understand why you feel that way.

A. You know, I've been thinking.
B. What?
A. I regret/I'm sorry _____.
   I wish _____.
B. What makes you say that?
A. If _____ , _____.
B. I can understand why you feel that way.

Now create an original scene with your partner. You can use the model above as a guide, but feel free to adapt and expand it any way you wish.

Listening: *Conclusions*

Listen and choose the best conclusion.

1. a. He got a B in the course.
   b. He didn't flunk the test.
   c. He didn't get a B in the course.

2. a. He has no trouble with his finances.
   b. He never took an accounting course.
   c. He regrets taking an accounting course.

3. a. She has a business degree.
   b. There aren't many opportunities for people with business degrees.
   c. She's having a problem finding a job.

4. a. She didn't make chocolate chip cookies.
   b. She didn't go to the supermarket.
   c. She bought some brown sugar.

5. a. Henry's plane has landed.
   b. Henry hasn't called yet.
   c. Mary thinks Henry is not going to call when the plane lands.

6. a. The cake must have been good.
   b. There wasn't any cake left over.
   c. There was some leftover cake.

Vocabulary Check: *Synonyms*

Choose the best synonym for the first word.

1. *option*   a. regret   b. choice   c. problem
2. *uneasy*   a. difficult   b. forced   c. uncomfortable
3. *embezzling*   a. funding   b. imbibing   c. stealing
4. *mall*   a. a business   b. a shopping area c. a parking area
5. to *evict*   a. to force out   b. to give up   c. to require
6. *to convert*   a. to open   b. to change   c. to expose
7. *to break up*   a. to separate   b. to be evident   c. to go out of business
8. *recourse*   a. evidence   b. alternative   c. replay
9. *to skip*   a. to jump   b. to slip   c. to miss
10. *to figure out* a. to draw   b. to understand   c. to move out
11. *to lay off*   a. to let go   b. to put down   c. to postpone

Studying English

The person on the previous page regrets not starting to study English when he was a young child. He thinks that if he had, he wouldn't be having so much trouble with pronunciation.

Ask other students in your class about their experiences.

When did you start studying English?
Do you wish you had started when you were young? Why?
What do you find most difficult about English?
What do you find easiest?

As a class, discuss the results of your interviews.

Here are the expressions you practiced in Chapter 8. Try to use as many as you can to expand your vocabulary and to add variety to your use of English.

Regret

It's a shame (that) _____.
It's a pity (that) _____.
I'm disappointed (that) _____.
It's disappointing (that) _____.
It's too bad (that) _____.
[less formal]
Too bad.

I regret (that) I _____.
I'm sorry (that) I _____.
I regret _____ing.
I'm sorry about _____ing.

I wish I hadn't _____ed.

Agreement/Disagreement

Expressing Agreement

I agree (with you).
You're right.
That's right.
That's true.
I know.

That's exactly what I was thinking.
That's exactly what I think.
That's just what I was thinking.
[less formal]
You can say that again!
You took the words right out of my
  mouth!

Me, too.
I think so, too.
I feel the same way.

Under the circumstances, I can see
  _____.
Given the circumstances, I can see
  _____.
Given the situation, I can see _____.

Wish–Hope

I wish *it were cheaper.*

I wish I could _____.
If only I could _____.

I was hoping _____.

Denying/Admitting

Admitting

The truth is . . .

The fact of the matter is . . .

I made a terrible mistake!
[less formal]
I (really) goofed!
I (really) blew it!

It's all my fault!
I'm entirely to blame!

Deduction

It looks like _____.
It seems like _____.
It seems as if _____.
It seems as though _____.

Satisfaction/Dissatisfaction

Inquiring about . . .

How are you enjoying _____?

Expressing Dissatisfaction

I'm not enjoying _____ (at all).

Sympathizing

That's too bad!
That's a shame!
That's a pity!
What a shame!
What a pity!
That's terrible!
That's awful!
I'm sorry to hear that.

Initiating a Topic

You know what I wish?

I've been meaning to ask you.
I keep forgetting to ask you.
I keep meaning to ask you.

(You know,) I've been thinking . . .

Clarification

Asking for Clarification

Do you mean (to say) _____?
Are you saying _____?
Does that mean _____?

Remembering/Forgetting

Indicating . . .

I forgot to _____.

Asking for and Reporting Information

What makes you say that?

9

COMMUNICATION STRATEGIES:
CLARIFYING
INTERRUPTING
REDIRECTING A CONVERSATION
ASSERTING OPINIONS

Two strangers are making *small talk* in the elevator. What do you think they're saying to each other?

Wendy needs to interrupt a business meeting that Doris is having with Richard. What do you think Wendy is saying, and how are Doris and Richard responding?

(1) Pardon me?
Pardon?
Excuse me?
What did you say?
What was that?
Come again?

(2) saying (that)
commenting (that)

A. Nice day today, isn't it.
B. **Pardon me?**(1)
A. I was just **saying**(2) it's a nice day today.
B. Oh, yes. It is.

1.
Looks like it's going to rain, . . .

2.
It sure is warm in here, . . .

3.
There sure are a lot of people shopping today, . . .

4.
The subway is pretty crowded tonight, . . .

5.
They sure don't give you a lot of leg-room between these seats, . . .

Strike up a conversation with a stranger.

Grammar Check: *Short Answers*

Choose the appropriate line for Speaker B.

	A	**B**
1.	Today was really a wonderful day!	a. Yes, it is. (b.) Yes, it was. c. Yes, it has been.
2.	Will you be studying Chinese while you're in Beijing?	(a.) Yes, I will. b. Yes, I'll be. c. Yes, I am going to.
3.	It's hard to resist those chocolate desserts.	a. I know. It was. b. You're right. It has. (c.) That's true. It is.
4.	They sure don't give you much food at this restaurant!	(a.) You're right. They don't. b. I know. It doesn't. c. No. You don't.
5.	I was just saying we need some rain.	a. Yes, it is. (b.) Yes, we do. c. Yes, I was.

Listening: *The Best Response*

Listen and choose the best response.

1. a. Yes, it is.
    b. Yes, it will.
    (c.) Yes, it does.

2. a. Yes, he did.
    b. Yes, he has.
    c. Yes, he was.

3. a. No, they hadn't.
    b. No, they weren't.
    c. No, they aren't.

4. a. Yes, I do.
    b. Yes, I am.
    c. Yes, I can.

5. a. No, I didn't.
    b. No, I don't.
    c. No, it wasn't.

6. a. Yes, she does.
    b. Yes, it is.
    c. Yes, they are.

7. a. You're right. It is.
    b. I know. They do.
    c. Yes, they are.

8. a. No, you won't!
    b. No, you aren't!
    c. No, I don't!

9. a. Yes, we will be.
    b. Yes, it will.
    c. Yes, we will.

InterCultural Connections

Talking to Strangers

The conversations on the previous page are typical ways in which Americans might *make conversation* with strangers. Would this happen in YOUR country? Do strangers often strike up conversations? If they do, what things might they say? Give some examples.

Look at that man! He's cutting in line!

annoying

A. **Doesn't it bother you when people**[1] cut in line?
B. Yes. **To me,**[2] cutting in line is very annoying.
A. It sure is.

Look at those people! They're throwing litter all over the park!

inconsiderate

A. **I can't stand it when people**[3] throw litter all over the park.
B. I know. **To me,**[2] throwing litter all over the park is very inconsiderate.
A. It sure is.

[1] Doesn't it bother you when people _____?
Aren't you annoyed when people _____?
Don't you (just) hate it when people _____?

[less formal]
Doesn't it get to you when people _____?
Wouldn't you like to clobber people who _____?

[2] To me,
As far as I'm concerned,

[less formal]
In my book,

[3] I can't stand it when people _____.
It really bothers me when people _____.

[more informal]
I can't take it when people _____.

Look at that man! He's smoking in the elevator!

rude

1.

Look at that customer! He's complaining about every little thing!

obnoxious

2. really hateful can not talk to someone

Look at that young man! He's refusing to give up his seat to a senior citizen!

selfish

3.

Look at that woman! She's parking in an area reserved for the handicapped!

thoughtless

4.

Look at those people! They're kissing in public!

tacky

5.

Express your disgust about something.

Function Check: *What's the Expression?*

1. In my _____, going out alone at night can be very dangerous.
   a. concern
   b. consideration
   (c.) book

2. I can't _____ when people crack their knuckles in public.
   (a.) stand it
   b. clobber them
   c. get to it

3. As far as I'm _____, people who speak out of turn in class are impolite.
   a. thinking
   (b.) concerned
   c. annoyed

4. _____, people who own fancy cars are ostentatious.
   a. I'm concerned
   b. I can't stand them
   (c.) To me

5. I can't _____ when people litter on the street.
   a. annoy it
   b. bother it
   (c.) take it

6. Doesn't it _____ when the boss yells at you?
   (a.) clobber you
   b. take it
   c. get to you

7.

Don't you just _____ it when people brag about themselves?
   a. annoy
   b. hate
   (c.) bother

Listening: *What's the Meaning?*

Listen and choose the answer that is closest in meaning to the sentence you have heard.

1. a. In my opinion, joining the union is a big mistake.
   b. My book says that it was a mistake to start the union.
   (c.) To me, it is essential that people join the union.

2. a. Doesn't it get to you when people don't show up at the tennis court?
   b. Aren't you annoyed when people don't get off the tennis court?
   c. Doesn't it bother you when people show off on the tennis court?

3. a. Doesn't it get to you when someone questions an answer you've just given?
   b. Don't you just hate it when someone asks you to repeat an answer you've just given?
   c. Aren't you annoyed when one person gives all the answers to the questions you've just asked?

4. a. Doesn't it annoy you when people tell you to do the dishes in the sink?
   b. Doesn't it bother you when people leave you with thirty dishes in the sink?
   c. Aren't you annoyed when people leave dirty dishes overnight in the sink?

Which of the things on page 154 bother you most?
What other things about people's behavior in public bother you?

A. The X-rays suggest that an extraction is indicated.
B. **I'm afraid I'm not following you.**[1]
A. Okay. **Let me put it this way:**[2] I'm going to have to pull your tooth.
B. Oh. **I understand.**[3]

[1] [less direct]
I'm afraid I'm not following you.
I'm not really sure what you're getting at.
I'm not quite clear as to what you mean (by that).

[more direct]
What do you mean (by that)?
What does that mean?
Could you clarify that (for me)?

[2] Let me put it this way:
Let me put it another way:
What I'm (really) saying is,
What I'm trying to say is,
What I mean is,
What I'm getting at is,
In other words,

[less formal]
Let me try that again.
Let me try that one more time.

[3] I understand.
I follow you.
I see.

1. "The war ended."

2. "You're fired."

3. "I think we should break up."

4. "The bookkeeper is going to quit."

5. "I'm going to have a baby."

Ask somebody for clarification.

Listening: *Who Are They?*

Listen and decide what the relationship between the two people is.

1. a. patient–doctor
    b. businessman–client
    c. doctor–patient *(c circled)*

2. a. nurse–head nurse
    b. mother–daughter
    c. housekeeper–homeowner

3. a. car dealer–customer
    b. husband–wife
    c. mechanic–customer

4. a. paper carrier–customer
    b. student–teacher
    c. office manager–secretary

5. a. architect–landlord
    b. tenant–tenant
    c. landlord–tenant

6. a. director–actor
    b. zookeeper–lion tamer
    c. telephone operator–customer

Reading: *"Bureaucratese" and Obfuscation*

Governmental double talk, or "bureaucratese" as it is sometimes called, is common in many countries, including the United States. Because certain situations call for a degree of formality or because government officials and spokespeople may not want to address an issue or respond to a question directly, overly complex language is often used that, on some occasions, is almost impossible to understand.

Presidential speeches and news reports are full of confusing rhetoric. The president may announce his decision "after long consideration of the pros and cons to postpone discussion of the matter until a more suitable time." In other words, he'll talk about it later! Or he may want to "communicate our most sincere desire to participate in the massive efforts to eliminate aggression and promote political stability in troubled areas of the world," or, simply stated, work toward peace.

Much of the time politicians promise their constituencies that they will attempt to "influence the administration to decrease the necessity of funds generated by internal revenue" (try to lower taxes), while "contributing toward the augmentation of the quality of life" (raising the standard of living). Sometimes, though, despite "their most fervent efforts to avoid inflationary government spending, the necessity of generating new revenue arises" (raising taxes is inevitable). When election year rolls around again, these public servants promise to "serve the public with increased and renewed energy" (keep doing their jobs) if the people will "show by their balloting their appreciation of past performance" (reelect them).

Obfuscation is at its peak when government officials want to avoid answering critical questions during press conferences. A simple query such as "Are we really going to invade Grenomia?" can prompt a rush of diplomatic doubletalk. "Immediate action will be taken only if circumstances warrant it. In that case, we have several contingency plans, one of which will be put into effect depending upon the seriousness of the situation." ARE we going to invade Grenomia? No one knows for sure. Government spokespeople make certain that their seemingly clear answers purposefully obscure messages.

In Your Own Words

For fun, choose a topic currently being talked about on TV or in the newspapers, and write about it in two ways: first, in clear, *normal*, language, and then in bureaucratic language filled with *double talk!* Compare your two versions with other students' creations!

(1) What you're (really) saying is
What you're trying to say is
What you mean is
In other words

(2) Don't jump to conclusions!
Don't read too much into
what I'm saying!

A. Your new sport jacket is a very unusual color.
B. **What you're really saying is**(1) you don't like it.
A. Come on, now! **Don't jump to conclusions!**(2) I didn't say I didn't like it. I just said it was a very unusual color.
B. Oh.

Function Check: *What's My Line?*

Choose the appropriate line for Speaker B.

	A	**B**
1.	It was very bold of you to tell the boss he needed to change his attitude.	_____ is I shouldn't have said it. a. What I meant to say b. What you're really saying ⓑ c. What I'm trying to say
2.	You don't like the walnut soufflé I spent five hours making?	Now don't _____! a. read too much b. conclude so fast c. jump to conclusions
3.	So you're saying you don't trust me?	Not at all. _____. a. In other words, you're right. b. Don't read too much into what I'm saying. c. You're right. Jump to conclusions.
4.	You new hair color is . . . different!	_____ you don't like it. a. What you say is b. What you're meaning is c. What you're trying to say is

Listening: *What's the Meaning?*

Listen and choose the answer that is closest in meaning to the sentence you have heard.

1. a. So you're really trying to spend all the money I gave you?
   b. So you're saying you gave away all the money you saved?
   c. In other words, the money I gave you is spent. ⓒ

2. a. Do you mean that you're trying to think, Captain?
   b. Do you mean that we're going under, Captain?
   c. Are you saying that they're singing to the Captain?

3. a. You mean you're sick and tired of spending so much?
   b. You're saying that you don't spend much time doing paperwork?
   c. You mean you're tired of doing so much paperwork?

4. a. You're trying to say that you don't know how to play that song?
   b. In other words, you can't play that long?
   c. You're saying that song isn't in that play?

InterChange

Technical Jargon

Every field (for example, business, computers, medicine) has its own *technical jargon*—specialized vocabulary used in that discipline. Find examples in newspapers and magazines or by talking to professionals in different areas. Then *teach* these words to other students in the class.

(1) Excuse me for interrupting,
Forgive me for interrupting,
(I'm) sorry for interrupting,
(I'm) sorry to interrupt,

(2) Wait a minute!
Hold on (a minute)!

(3) Did you say
Was that

A. **Excuse me for interrupting,**(1) but you have an important call on line 5.
B. Thank you. Oh. **Wait a minute!**(2) **Did you say**(3) line 9?
A. No. Line 5.
B. Thanks.

1.
2.
3.
4.
5.

* I.R.S.: Internal Revenue Service.
C.I.A.: Central Intelligence Agency.

Listening: *Conclusions*

Listen and choose the best conclusion.

1. a. Mr. Mason is waiting at the door.
   b. Mr. Gleason is being interrupted.
   c. Mr. Mason is on the phone. *(circled)*

2. a. The president's secretary wants to see him.
   b. The Secretary of State is with the president in his office.
   c. The Secretary of State wants to see the president.

3. a. They are inside the tallest skyscraper in the city.
   b. The building has thirty-four floors.
   c. The building has forty-four floors.

4. a. They're having a conversation while they're eating lunch.
   b. Brunch is about to be served.
   c. Lunch is about to be served.

Function Check: *What's My Line?*

Choose the appropriate line for Speaker B.

	A	B
1.	Sorry to interrupt, but your husband is on the phone.	a. You're excused. b. I'm sorry. c. Did you say my husband? *(circled)*
2.	Excuse me, sir, but I've got those bills you wanted.	a. Give me those pills. b. Sorry for interrupting. c. Was that bills or pills?
3.	That number is 783–9604.	a. I'm sorry to interrupt. b. Thank you. Oh, wait a minute. Was that 9604? c. Excuse me for interrupting.
4.	I'm sorry to interrupt, but there's a bomb scare, and everyone must evacuate the building immediately!	a. Excuse me for interrupting. b. Forgive me. c. Hold on! Did you say a bomb?

InterChange

With a partner, discuss when it is appropriate to interrupt a conversation. What signs should you look for before interrupting? When is it inappropriate to interrupt?

Then share your ideas with other students in the class. No interruptions, please!

the merger with the State Street Bank

The new Xerox machine arrived this morning.

A. **Regarding**[1] the merger with the State Street Bank, . . .
B. Oh. **By the way,**[2] the new Xerox machine arrived this morning.
A. Oh, I didn't know that. Now, **as I was saying,**[3] regarding the merger with the State Street Bank, **in my opinion,**[4] . . .
B. Excuse me for interrupting, but I'm afraid it's getting late. **I've really got to go now.**[5]
A. Oh. That's too bad. We haven't really had a chance to talk about the merger with the State Street Bank.
B. I know. I'm sorry. Let's continue the conversation soon.

[1] Regarding _____,
Regarding the issue of _____,
As far as _____ is concerned,

[2] By the way,
Incidentally,
Before I forget,
I don't mean to change the subject, but

[3] as I was saying, . . .
to get back to what I was saying, . . .
to get back to what we were talking about, . . .

[4] in my opinion,
as I see it,
the way I see it,
if you ask me,

[5] I've (really) got to go now.
I've (really) got to be going now.
I (really) have to go now.
I'd (really) better go now.
I (really) need to go now.
I (really) should go now.
I have to/I've got to run.
I have to/I've got to get going.

my request for maternity leave

We've ordered new uniforms for all the employees.

1.

my broken stove

I'm thinking of painting the front hallway.

2.

our plans to get married

My roommate, Sarah, just got a new job.

3.

my suggestion for increasing productivity

The supervisor on the night shift quit yesterday.

4.

Einstein's theory of relativity

Did you know that there's going to be a big dance this Saturday night?

5.

Change the subject of a conversation.

Function Check: *What's the Expression?*

1. Now, _____ our plans for the new office, I'd like to have a large window here so there's a lot of light.
   a. regarding the concern of
   b. regarding the issue of *(circled)*
   c. incidentally

2. Oh, _____, I wanted to tell you that your new business cards just arrived.
   a. before I forget
   b. in my opinion
   c. by the time

3. _____, we have to think very carefully before nominating our new vice-presidential candidate.
   a. To get back to what I see
   b. The thing to see is
   c. If you ask me

4. _____, did you notice that there's some mail for you in the mailbox?
   a. The way I see it
   b. By the way
   c. Oh, I don't mean to change

5. Well, _____, I think we should send Melissa to a public school instead of to a private school.
   a. as my mind sees it
   b. I don't mean to subject you, but
   c. to get back to what we were talking about

6. Well, _____, I'll call you later.
   a. to get back to what I was saying
   b. don't get going now
   c. I have to run

7.
   Sorry for interrupting, but _____.
   a. I really have to get to run now.
   b. I'd really better go now
   c. I've to get going now

Listening: *Conclusions*

Listen and choose the best conclusion.

1. a. Judy is having a baby.
   b. Judy is being interrupted. *(circled)*
   c. Judy didn't want to discuss the new sales strategy.

2. a. Jenny's car is in the shop.
   b. Jenny and Roger are planning their weekend.
   c. Roger can take his car this weekend.

3. a. Arthur thinks the sink needs repairing.
   b. Arthur's wife wants him to finish what he was saying.
   c. Arthur wanted to finish his conversation.

4. a. Liz wants to start off the meal with fruit salad.
   b. Jane knows where the place cards are.
   c. Liz is concerned about the place cards.

5. a. Peter just got a new blue and green tie.
   b. Peter's friend thinks his suit looks better with green.
   c. Peter doesn't want to show his new tie to his friend.

6. a. Professor Lawrence stressed the importance of promptness.
   b. The report is due next week.
   c. Professor Lawrence forgot when the report was due.

InterChange

What's your opinion? In each conversation on page 162, the second speaker changed the focus of the conversation. Why did the speaker do that? Do you think the person wanted to *avoid* the subject? Discuss with a partner, and then share and compare your thoughts with the rest of the class.

Two people are exchanging opinions. Practice this scene with a partner.

A. What's your opinion about nuclear energy?
B. Nuclear energy? Now, that's quite an issue! I actually have some pretty strong viewpoints regarding nuclear energy. Are you interested in hearing them?
A. Yes.
B. Well, in my opinion, nuclear energy is our best hope for the future.
A. But don't you think it poses a threat to the safety of the population?
B. Not really. As I see it, nuclear reactors are a clean and safe source of electricity.
A. Well, if you ask me, people don't realize how dangerous radiation can be.
B. The thing to keep in mind is that our oil and gas resources are limited. And furthermore, . . .
A. Let me say one more thing.
B. Okay.
A. I'd just like to point out that I think too many accidents are happening at nuclear power plants all over the country.
B. You know, we could probably go on talking about this forever and never come to an agreement.
A. You're probably right. I guess we just don't see eye to eye when it comes to nuclear energy.
B. I guess not.

A. What's your opinion about _____?
B. _____? Now, that's quite an issue! I actually have some pretty strong viewpoints regarding _____. Are you interested in hearing them?
A. Yes.
B. Well, in my opinion, _____
_____.
A. But don't you think _____
_____?
B. Not really. As I see it, _____
_____.
A. Well, if you ask me, _____
_____.
B. The thing to keep in mind is that _____
_____.
And furthermore, . . .
A. Let me say one more thing.
B. Okay.
A. I'd just like to point out that I think _____
_____.
B. You know, we could probably go on talking about this forever and never come to an agreement.
A. You're probably right. I guess we just don't see eye to eye when it comes to
_____.
B. I guess not.

Working with a partner, choose an issue, each take different sides of the issue, and list three good reasons for your opinions.

Issue: _____

Opinions
1. _____
_____
2. _____
_____
3. _____
_____

Opinions
1. _____
_____
2. _____
_____
3. _____
_____

Now create an original scene with your partner. Exchange your opinions. You can use the model above as a guide, but feel free to adapt and expand it any way you wish.

	A	**B**
1.	a. I need your advice on something b. I've really got to get going. ⓒ I hope you'll be able to join me for dinner.	I'd love to.
2.	a. It was nice meeting you. b. I hope you'll forgive me. c. I don't think I've ever seen a better performance.	Thank you for the compliment.
3.	a. Can I take a message? b. I wouldn't be concerned about him. c. Would you please remind me to call him tomorrow?	I'm not so sure about that.
4.	a. Would you mind taking me to the station? b. I'm sure I'd be able to learn quickly. c. Let me say one more thing.	No, not at all.
5.	a. That's too bad. b. It completely slipped my mind. c. Something bad must have happened.	Don't jump to conclusions.
6.	a. No trouble at all. b. It would be my pleasure. c. I really appreciate it.	Don't mention it. *devada no és de que*
7.	a. Perhaps you have some questions about the application? b. Would you be willing to help me with my science project? c. Would I have to get approval from my supervisor?	Yes, it's mandatory.
8.	a. I've got something scheduled for Friday night. b. It's a shame we can't get together. c. Let's keep in touch.	I feel the same way.

9.	a. You'd better get out of the way! b. I hope you'll come to the meeting. c. I wouldn't go as far as that.	Thanks for the warning.

10.	I think there's too much prejudice in the world today.	That's _____ what I think.
		    a. a pity
		    b. the same
		    c. exactly

11.	Don't worry about not being able to take me sailing.	I feel terrible. I'm not one _____.
		    a. to speak out of turn
		    b. to go back on my word
		    c. get out of it

12.	You have to work late again?	I'm sorry. There's _____ I can do about it.
		    a. nothing
		    b. no way
		    c. much

13.	Let's go to the new Thai restaurant.	Good idea. _____ it's wonderful.
		    a. You have a point
		    b. People say
		    c. I insist

14.	I think you should settle your argument in court.	I _____ you're right.
		    a. advise
		    b. suggest
		    c. guess

15.	I've decided to keep my apartment through the winter.	Well, under the _____, I can see why you'd want to do that.
		    a. advice
		    b. circumstances
		    c. mistake

16.	How _____ to go waterskiing on Sunday? a. would you be able b. are you supposed c. would you like	That sounds terrific.
17.	I'm _____ this opportunity to meet with you. a. grateful for b. helpful for c. annoyed with	If I can help you in any other way, please let me know.

Here are the expressions you practiced in Chapter 9. Try to use as many as you can to expand your vocabulary and to add variety to your use of English.

Focusing Attention

To me, . . .
As far as I'm concerned, . . .
In my opinion, . . .
As I see it, . . .
The way I see it, . . .
If you ask me, . . .
[less formal]
In my book, . . .

(And) furthermore, . . .

Let me say one more thing.

I'd (just) like to point out that . . .

The thing to keep in mind is that . . .

Directing/Redirecting a Conversation

By the way, . . .
Incidentally, . . .
Before I forget, . . .
I don't mean to change the subject, but . . .

Now . . .

As I was saying, . . .
To get back to what I was saying, . . .
To get back to what we were talking about, . . .

Interrupting

Excuse me for interrupting, (but) . . .
Forgive me for interrupting, (but) . . .
(I'm) sorry for interrupting, (but) . . .
(I'm) sorry to interrupt, (but) . . .

Initiating a Topic

Regarding _____, . . .
Regarding the issue of _____, . . .
As far as _____ is concerned, . . .

Initiating Conversations

Nice day today, isn't it.

Clarification

Asking for Clarification

[less direct]
I'm afraid I'm not following you.
I'm not really sure what you're getting at.
I'm not quite clear as to what you

mean (by that).

[more direct]
What do you mean (by that)?
What does that mean?
Could you clarify that (for me)?

Giving Clarification

Let me put it this way: . . .
Let me put it another way: . . .
What I'm (really) saying is, . . .
What I'm trying to say is, . . .
What I mean is, . . .
What I'm getting at is, . . .
In other words, . . .
[less formal]
Let me try that again.
Let me try that one more time.

What you're (really) saying is . . .
What you're trying to say is . . .
What you mean is . . .
In other words . . .

I didn't say _____.

I just said _____.

Checking and Indicating Understanding

Checking One's Own Understanding

Did you say _____?
Was that _____?

Indicating Understanding

(Now) { I understand. / I follow you. / I see.

Asking for Repetition

Pardon me?
Pardon?
Excuse me?
What did you say?
What was that?
Come again?

Complaining

Doesn't it bother you when people _____?
Aren't you annoyed when people _____?
Don't you (just) hate it when

people _____?

[less formal]
Doesn't it get to you when people _____?
Wouldn't you like to clobber people who _____?

_____ (ing) is (very) annoying/ inconsiderate/rude/obnoxious/ selfish/thoughtless/tacky.

I can't stand it when people _____.
It really bothers me when people _____.
[less formal]
I can't take it when people _____.

Agreement/Disagreement

Expressing Agreement

Yes.
I know.

It sure is.

I _____ either.

You're (probably) right.

Expressing Disagreement

But don't you think _____?

Not really.

We don't see eye to eye when it comes to _____.

Correcting

No. *Line 5.*

Leave Taking

(I'm afraid) it's getting late.

I've (really) got to go (now).
I've (really) got to be going (now).
I (really) have to go (now).
I'd (really) better go (now).
I (really) need to go (now).
I (really) should go (now).
I have to run.
I have to get going.
I've got to run.
I've got to get going.

These scenes review the functions and conversation strategies in Chapters, 7, 8, and 9. Who do you think these people are? What do you think they're talking about? With other students, improvise conversations based on these scenes and act them out.

1.

2.

3.

4.

5.

6.

7.

8.

Chapter 1

Page 2: "Would You Like to Go to the Zoo?"

- In line 3, Speaker A says, "Me neither." This is a short conversational response meaning "I haven't either" or "Neither have I."

Exercises

4: Going for a drive in the country is a popular form of recreation.

5: Fruit farmers often allow the public to pick fruit. People pay a small fee to pick the fruit as a form of recreation and then take the fruit home.

Page 4: "Would You by Any Chance Be Interested in Seeing a Movie?"

- The expressions " Would you (by any chance) be interested in _____ing?" and "You wouldn't (by any chance) be interested in _____ing, would you?" are indirect and allow the person being invited to decline politely.
- "College entrance exams." To be accepted into an American college or university, students usually need to take college entrance (or "college board") examinations.
- In line 5, Speaker A expresses disappointment when he says "That's too bad."
- In line 6, Speaker B thanks Speaker A for the invitation. Saying "Thank you" when declining an invitation is always appropriate and expected.
- Speaker B suggests that they see a movie "some other time." This is a typical expression used when declining an invitation.

Exercises

2: "Spring cleaning." After a long winter, people often set aside some time to clean the inside and outside of their homes very well.

5: "Miniature golf." A popular form of recreation, miniature golf is similar to the game of golf but is played in a very small area.

Page 6: "Can You Come?"

- "Company picnic." Large and small businesses often have an annual picnic for employees and their families or guests.
- Speaker A really wants Speaker B to come to the company picnic. In line 5, she urges him to come by asking "Is there any chance you could possibly get out of working overtime?"
- "Get out of" = avoid the responsibility of doing something.
- Speaker A is complimenting Speaker B in line 8 when she says "It won't be much of a company picnic without you!" She is saying that Speaker B will be greatly missed if he doesn't come.
- "Get back to" = give an answer at a later time.
- "Not be much of a" = not be very successful.
- "Do one's best" = try very hard.

Exercises

1: "Slumber party." Young girls and boys often have parties where friends come to sleep overnight.

3: "Throw a party" = have a party.

4: "Put together a game" = organize a game.

5: "Pot luck supper." This is a common type of party where each guest brings something that he or she has cooked at home. "Pot luck" means that any combination of food is possible.

Page 8: "We'd Like to Invite You and Your Wife Over for Dinner"

- In line 9, Speaker A says, "How does 7:00 sound?" Asking if a certain time is all right is a polite way of naming a time.

Exercises

1: "Brunch" = a combination of breakfast and lunch, usually eaten on Sundays.

2: "Barbecue" = a meal cooked outdoors over a fire.

5: "Get-together" = a small, informal party.

Page 10: "I Think I Should Be Going Now"

- These speakers have been talking for some time. In line 1, Speaker A marks the end of this conversation by saying "Well" and initiates the leave-taking ritual.
  1. Both speakers express pleasure at having seen one another.
     "It's been really nice seeing you again."
     "I'm glad we bumped into each other."
  2. Both speakers say they need to leave.
     "I think I should be going now."
     "I should get going, too."
  3. Reasons for leaving are given.
     "I need to have this car back at the rental agency by 2:00."
  4. Promises to see one another again are made.
     "Let's get together soon."
     "Okay. I'll call you."
  5. The speakers finally say their actual good-byes.
  In the United States, the leave-taking process almost always includes the above steps.
- In line 3, Speaker A's saying that he is going to leave ("You know . . .") serves to make the announcement less direct and, therefore, more polite.
- By saying "Actually" in line 5, Speaker B is really saying "Now that you've brought up the subject of leaving, I should leave, too."

Page 12: "I've Really Got to Go Now"

- The speakers have been talking for some time. When Speaker A says "By the way," she redirects the conversation to the topic of time and taking leave.
- In "You'd better hurry!," "had better" is a strong suggestion or recommendation.
- The expression "(I'll) see you soon/later/tomorrow/next week/. . ." is not a promise or commitment of any kind. It is simply part of the leave-taking process.

Pages 14–15: Communicators

- The speakers have been talking for some time. When Speaker A says "I'd love to continue this conversation, but . . . ," she is setting the scene for the beginning of the leave-taking process.
- In line 2, "Well," indicates that Speaker B understands the situation and is also ready to begin the leave-taking process.
- In line 15, when Speaker A says "You know," she is politely reminding Speaker B of her need to leave.

Chapter 2

Page 20: "I've Had a Lot of Experience Taking Shorthand"

- In line 3, "Then" is equivalent to "Therefore," "In that case," or "So."
- In line 3, Speaker A asks a question using a declarative sentence with question intonation. This form is commonly used when an affirmative answer is expected.
- In line 5, the job candidate does not want to be too direct. She wants to show confidence and also humility. This is why she responds "I would say so."

Page 21: "I Haven't Altered Men's Clothing Before"

- Because it is very important to show ability and confidence at a job interview, Speaker B tells what she IS able to do, rather than simply saying "No" to the interviewer's question.

Pages 24–25: "I'm Afraid I Wasn't Able to Do It"

- In lines 1 and 3, Speaker A is preparing Speaker B for the bad news: first by warning him that he will be disappointed, and then by reminding Speaker B of what he had asked Speaker A to do.
- In line 3, "Well" is used to hesitate briefly and call attention to the information that will follow.
- In line 4, Speaker B has clearly been prepared for bad news as he tentatively asks "Yes?"
- In line 6, Speaker B's "Oh?" is a way of asking for an explanation.
- Speaker B is very understanding in this situation. He tells Speaker A not to worry about what happened. In line 10, he says, "These things happen." This indicates that he completely excuses Speaker A and has no bad feelings toward him.
- Speaker A is very apologetic and checks to be sure that Speaker B understands the situation by asking "You aren't upset?"

Exercises

8: "Booked" = full.
9: "Blind date." When a man and a woman arrange to go on a date before having met each other, it is a "blind date." "Slip one's mind" = forget.

Page 28: "I Won't Be Able to Go Bowling with You"

- "What's up?" is a very informal expression used to ask for information.
- Lines 1 and 2 indicate that the speakers are good friends and had been talking on the phone earlier that day.
- In line 3 "I'm afraid" indicates that the speaker regrets what will follow.
- In line 8, "No problem" is short for "It's no problem" and indicates that Speaker B understands Speaker A's dilemma and doesn't mind.

Exercises

2: Fever "breaks" when the body temperature begins to return to normal.

Page 30: "I Didn't Know That Was Required"

- In line 3, Speaker A is surprised by what Speaker B has said and asks Speaker B to repeat the new information she has heard when she asks "Have I had it what?!"
- Throughout this conversation the passive voice is used. This is typical when a source of authority (the agent) is either not known or not important.
- In line 7, Speaker A expresses surprise when she says "Oh."

Exercises

2: A Notary Public is a person empowered by law to certify the authenticity of certain documents. He or she signs and stamps (notarizes) these papers.
5: When two people share a bank account, it is called a "joint" bank account.

Pages 32–33: Communicators

- In lines 2 and 5, Speaker B says "All right" and "I understand" to show that he is listening to and understands what Speaker A is saying.
- When Speaker A says "Now" in line 12, she is changing the focus of attention from herself to the interviewee.
- In line 28, Speaker B initiates the leave-taking process by saying "I've probably taken up enough of your time."
- In line 29, "be in touch with" = contact by phone or by letter.

Chapter 3

Page 38: "Please Clean Up Your Room Before Dinner"

- Saying a person's name is a common way to attract his or her attention.
- The requests "Please _____," "Can you (please) _____," "Will you (please) _____," "Would you (please) _____," "I'd like you to _____," and "I wish you would _____" are polite and informal and are used between people who know each other well.

Exercises

1: "Roll up" the windows means to close the car windows.

Page 39: "Please Retype the Letter to Mr. Casey"

- Repeating back information with question intonation is a common way of checking understanding ("The letter to Mr. Casey?").
- In line 3, "While you're at it" means "at the same time."
- The responses "Certainly" and "Of course" are appropriate when speaking to a person of authority.

Exercises

5: "The Today Show" is a popular TV morning news program in the United States. Famous people are interviewed on this type of program.

Pages 42–43: "Could You Do Me a Favor?"

- "Could you do me a favor?" is a polite way to preface a request.
- The expressions for requests in these model dialogs are polite and are used when asking someone to do something you consider important.
- In line 5 (Model 2), Speaker B responds to Speaker A's request by saying "No, I wouldn't mind." He is actually saying "yes" to the request because he is responding negatively to the question "Would you mind _____?"

Exercises

5: "Keep an eye on" = watch for problems.

Pages 46–47: "I Was Wondering if You'd Be Willing to Switch Seats with Me?"

- "Excuse me" is a very polite way of attracting someone's attention.
- In line 4, Speaker A hesitates, "Uh . . . yes" while thinking of what to say next.
- In line 7, when Speaker A says "Thank you very much," he or she is relieved and very grateful to Speaker B.

Exercises

5: It is a common practice for waiters and waitresses in restaurants to sing "Happy Birthday" to customers who are celebrating birthdays.

Page 50: "I'd Like to, but I'm Afraid I Can't"

- Lines 1 and 3 are a common exchange involving requests. In line 3, Speaker B is expressing regret when he says "Gee." When saying no to a request, Americans usually say, "I'd like to, but I can't."
- In line 5, Speaker A acknowledges and accepts Speaker B's response to his request when he says "Oh, okay."
- People generally feel badly when they have to refuse a request. In line 6, Speaker B clearly feels badly and apologizes ("I'm really sorry").

Exercises

4: A "Little League" team is a baseball team made up of children.
5: Fifty-five miles per hour is the maximum speed limit on most U.S. highways. (The police officer in Exercise 5 regrets having to give a speeding ticket and by explaining is being extremely polite about why she must give one to this person.)

Page 52: Communicators

- The form of this telephone conversation is very common.

1. The caller initiates the conversation by saying "Hello."
2. The caller asks to speak to someone.
3. The person answering the phone tells the caller the person is not at home.
4. The person answering the phone asks if he or she can take a message.
5. The caller says yes and identifies himself or herself.
6. The caller gives the message to the person answering the phone.
7. The person answering the phone says that he or she will convey the message.
8. The caller expresses gratitude.
9. The speakers say good-bye.

- In line 6, Speaker A asks, "Is that it?" This expression means "Is that everything?"
- In line 7, Speaker B says, "I guess so." This is a less direct way of saying "Yes."
- In the United States, a friend is often asked to bring food or beverages to a party given by a close friend.

Chapter 4

Page 60: "Do You Have Any Suggestions?"

- In line 3, the pharmacist repeats "a fresh-tasting toothpaste" to show that she's thinking about the question being asked.
- The expressions "Everybody says . . .," "Everybody tells me . . .," "People say . . .," "Most people say . . .," "They say . . .," and "I hear . . ." are used when reporting generally known information.

Page 62: "How About Going Window-Shopping?"

- In line 3, Speaker A begins to make a suggestion by saying "Well." This makes the suggestion that follows less direct and more open to discussion.
- In line 4, Speaker B prefaces her negative response by saying "Oh, I don't know." By being less direct, she is softening the negative answer to come.
- In line 5, Speaker B says, "Any other suggestions?" This is a shorthand form of the question "Do you have any other suggestions?"

Page 64: "I Strongly Advise You"

- Speaker A is an authority figure in this situation and makes her advice very strong when she says in line 1, "As your guidance counselor."
- The expressions "I (strongly) advise you to _____," "I urge you to _____," "I recommend that you _____," and "I recommend _____ing" are strong, authoritative ways of giving advice.
- In line 3, Speaker B questions Speaker A's advice because, in this case, she really does not want to take Physics!
- In line 6, Speaker B finally accepts this new information when she says "Oh."

Exercises
5: "Lose your shirt" = lose all of your money or investments.

Page 66: "Can I Offer You Some Advice?"

- "You seem troubled/upset" and "You don't seem to be yourself today" are expressions used by a person who knows another person well. Speaker A recognizes that Speaker B has a problem and expresses concern when he asks about the problem.
- The expression "Is anything the matter/wrong/ bothering you?" is a common way of asking a friend to be truthful about how he or she feels.
- Because it is important to be very tactful when giving advice, Speaker A uses the indirect "Well", and asks if he can offer some advice in line 4.

Exercises
1: "Security deposit." In the United States, when a tenant agrees to rent an apartment, the landlord may require a

security deposit. This money is to be returned when the tenant moves out.
3: "To harass" means to annoy or bother. It has also become a legal term to connote inappropriate innuendoes—both verbal and physical—toward a co-worker in one's place of employment.
4: "Burning me out." To become burnt out means that an activity or responsibility is causing too much pressure or stress. "Take a few days off" = take time away from work.
5: "Level with" = tell someone the truth.

Pages 68–69: "I Need Your Advice on Something"

- The two speakers are friends. It is usually a friend, or someone known well, who is asked for this kind of advice.
- The expressions in this model dialog are less direct ways of offering suggestions when someone asks for advice.
- In the last line of the conversation, Speaker A says, "Hmm. I hadn't thought of that." This means that she thinks Speaker B's advice is good and she will think seriously about doing what Speaker B suggests.
- It is becoming increasingly common for mothers of young children to work outside the home. While a mother works, the child often stays at a child-care center in the care of professional child-care workers.

Exercises
2: "Be fed up with"= be very tired of and ready to stop something.
3: "Weight Watchers" is a club for overweight people who wish to lose weight.
5: "Have it" = be very tired of something and ready to stop.
7: In the United States, many people consult a psychiatrist or therapist when feeling depressed.
8: The U.S. military helps pay for the college education of those who enlist.
9: "Be at each other's throats" means that two people are very annoyed with each other.

Page 72: "Thanks for the Warning"

- The expressions "(Be) careful!," "Look out!," and "Watch out!" are used to warn someone of an immediate danger.
- The situations in Model 1 and Model 2 could both result in injury. In such situations, it is common and acceptable to use the imperative form "Careful!"
- In the first model, Speaker B quickly answers, "Huh?" in line 2. This informal response is appropriate because the person responding is surprised and caught off guard.
- In line 4 of both models, Speaker B is asking Speaker A why something is dangerous when he or she says "Oh?"

Page 74: Communicators

- In line 10, Speaker B says, "Make it a point to." This expression means "Really try to."
- In line 13, Speaker B says "Oh" to signal that she has just remembered something important.

Chapter 5

Page 78: "I Agree"

- A tag question, such as "didn't we" in line 2, is often used to emphasize agreement.

Page 79: "That's Just What I Was Thinking"

Exercises
1: "Off key" = not in tune with the music.
4: "Corny" jokes are simple, often repeated, and not very funny.
5: "Up to something" = to be doing or planning to do something secretively.

Page 82: "That Might Be True"

- In line 2, Speaker B is tentatively agreeing with Speaker A ("That might be true"), but at the same time is expressing his own opinion: "However, . . . Wouldn't you agree that . . .?"
- In line 2, Speaker B uses a negative question because he wants and expects Speaker A to agree with his opinion.

Exercises
5: "Leaves a lot to be desired" is a polite way of saying that something is not very good and needs improvement.

Page 83: "I'm Afraid You're Right"

- In this conversation, Speaker A makes a personal observation about Speaker B. The two speakers are close friends and know each other well enough to be candid with one another. A good friend might also probe further to find out why a friend's behavior has changed by asking "Is anything wrong?" "Do you want to talk about it?" "Is everything okay?" "Is something bothering you?"
- In line 2, Speaker B reluctantly agrees with Speaker A's observation ("I'm afraid you're right") because she is not happy about the reality of the situation. At this point, she might offer some explanation about her changed behavior.
- In the United States, being quiet and withdrawn is often considered unusual behavior and may indicate that something is wrong.

Exercises
1 & 2: The first speaker's observation in these two exercises is acceptable only when made by a very close friend or relative. It would be extremely rude to make such an observation about a person you do not know well.

Page 86: "That Isn't Exactly Right"

- In this conversation, Speaker A is Speaker B's superior (his boss). Speaker B therefore corrects Speaker A with a very indirect expression ("Excuse me, Mr. Perkins, but . . . "), which makes the correction polite and acceptable.
- In line 5, Speaker A says, "Oh." He is indicating that he understands his mistake.

Page 88: "That's Not True"

- In this conversation, Speaker A is confronting Speaker B in a very direct way. The speakers are sisters, so Speaker A feels free to be very direct.
- The expressions "Come on!," "Look!," "Listen!," "Admit it!," and "Face it!" are informal ways of persuading someone.

Pages 90–91: Communicators

- Speaker A initiates this conversation with a negative question. She is assuming that Speaker B will agree with her opinion.
- In line 3, Speaker B indirectly (politely) disagrees with Speaker A's opinion by saying "I'm not so sure about that."
- In line 4, Speaker A shows surprise and asks for clarification when she says "Oh?"
- In line 5, Speaker B disagrees politely and expresses his own opinion on the topic.
- In the last line, Speaker A expresses disagreement and doubt when she says "Well."

Exercises
3: In the United States, the question of when young people are old enough to drink alcohol is a controversial one, and the legal age to purchase alcohol and to drink alcoholic beverages varies from state to state.

Chapter 6
Page 96: "I'm Positive"

- In the first model, the father of the bride is asking his daughter if she wants to "go through with this." Getting married is a big step, and the father wants his daughter to be absolutely sure of her decision.

Exercises
5: Sherlock Holmes is a fictitious British detective made famous in the mystery novels of Sir Arthur Conan Doyle.

Holmes's good friend, Doctor Watson, frequently aids him in solving mysterious crimes.

Page 98: "In All Likelihood"

- In line 3, Speaker A repeats Speaker B's response to his question as a way of showing interest in her decision.
- In line 3, Speaker A says "Oh" as he contemplates this new information.

Exercises
4: When girls turn sixteen years old, they frequently have a special "sweet sixteen" birthday party to which they invite both boys and girls.

5: A popular kind of TV show is the game show. On these programs, contestants can win large prizes if they answer questions correctly or make the right decisions.

Page 99: "It Should Arrive Any Minute Now"

- In line 2, Speaker B uses an expression of probability rather than certainty because, even though his response is probably correct, he can't be absolutely sure.
- In line 3, Speaker A is looking for reassurance when she repeats "Any minute now?"

Exercises
4: When a customer deposits a check in a bank, the check normally takes a period of time to "clear" (for funds to be transferred). Until the check clears, the customer usually does not have access to those funds.

Page 102: "She Must Have Gotten Stuck in Traffic"

- In line 2, "show up" = arrive.
- Speaker B keeps on trying to put Speaker A's mind at ease by forming intelligent hypotheses about why the teacher is late for class.
- In line 3, "get stuck" = be in a car and unable to move.
- In line 4, Speaker A says, "I don't know," meaning that he is not sure he agrees with Speaker B's idea.
- In line 6, Speaker B continues to try to stop Speaker A from worrying when she says "Oh, come on now."

Exercises
2: "Be tied up" = be busy.
3: "Lose track of time" = not be conscious of the time of day.
5: "Be caught up" = be entangled.

Page 104: "I Might Buy the Cheap One"

- In line 1, Speaker A uses the verb "purchase" when he approaches Speaker B. Salespeople use this word; in normal conversation, people usually use the verb "buy."
- In line 2, Speaker B is indirectly asking for advice when he expresses uncertainty.
- Normally it is impolite to use the imperative "Don't . . .!" (line 4) with strangers, but when it is prefaced with an expression such as "Take my advice," it is appropriate.
- In line 4, Speaker A advises and warns Speaker B when he says "Don't buy the cheap one! You'll be disappointed." In English, advice is frequently accompanied by a warning.

Exercises
3: A subcompact is a very small car.

Page 106: "It's a Possibility"

- In line 4, when Speaker B asks the negative tag question "You wouldn't REALLY quit your job, would you?," she is reinforcing her disbelief and surprise at Speaker A's intention.

Exercises
1: "Drop out." In the United States, if a young person does not complete the four years needed for a college degree, he or she "drops out."

5: "Run away from home and join the circus." Young children sometimes consider leaving home, and some actually do so if their home or family situation becomes very stressful. In earlier days, joining the circus was a common childhood fantasy.

Page 108: "There's Not Much Chance of That Happening"

Exercises

5: The speakers are talking about characters in an episode of a daily soap opera. This type of TV drama depicts the ongoing problems of its characters.

Page 110: Communicators

- In line 12, Speaker A doesn't understand that Speaker B is asking for advice, so he asks, "Excuse me?"
- Speaker A does not want to be too direct with his advice, so he hesitates and makes sure that Speaker B understands that he is only expressing his personal opinion.

Chapter 7
Page 116: "Good Job!"

- In line 2, Speaker B says, "Do you really think so?" This response indicates either that the speaker is being modest or that he is unsure of his accomplishment.
- In line 7, Speaker B thanks Speaker A for the compliment. Acknowledgment is expected when a compliment is given.

Page 118: "Do You Approve of the Way I Clipped Fifi's Hair?"

- In the United States, people do not generally like to criticize others. When expressing disapproval, it is important to be indirect and tactful. In this conversation, in line 2, Speaker B hesitates and prepares Speaker A for her disapproving words when she says "Can I be frank with you?" In line 4, Speaker B uses the passive voice to "soften" the criticism by making it a little less direct.
- In line 6, Speaker A politely accepts Speaker B's expression of disapproval and apologizes.

Exercises

5: In this situation, the pilot is being playful with the young passenger.

Page 120: "You Really Shouldn't Have Raised Your Voice to the Boss"

- In line 1, Speaker A makes it very clear that she does not want to insult or directly reprimand Speaker B. She wants to point out Speaker B's mistake as a favor to a friend.
- In line 3, by responding "Oh?" Speaker B is in fact asking "Do you really think so?"
- In line 5, to say that something is "not a good idea" is a very tactful way of expressing disapproval.
- In line 6, Speaker B says "Hmm" while thinking about the criticism that Speaker A has offered.

Page 121: "I Really Wish You Hadn't Removed the Coffee Machine"

- Speaker A initiates the topic of the coffee machine delicately because she does not wish to criticize her manager too directly. She does this by saying "I hate to say it, but."
- Speaker A expresses disapproval of Speaker B's action by pointing out the negative results of his action (employee morale is down).

Exercises

1: "Not sleep a wink" = not sleep at all.
4: "Laughing stock" = the object of ridicule.

Page 124: "I Apologize"

- In line 3, Speaker A draws attention to new information by introducing it with "You know."

Exercises

5: "Mess up" = make mistakes.

Page 125: "I Hope You'll Forgive Me"

Exercises

2: In some neighborhoods, the newspaper is delivered to the home. Traditionally, this was done by a young boy or girl on a bicycle. Increasingly, newspapers are delivered by adults in automobiles.
4: "Petty cash" = cash kept on hand by small businesses for minor expenses.

Page 128: "Maybe You Ought to Apologize"

- Speaker A (a mother) knows that Speaker B (her son) has hurt his father's feelings. While Speaker A doesn't actually suggest that Speaker B should apologize until the end of the conversation, this is the reason that Speaker A has brought up the entire subject.
- In the summertime in the United States, it is a tradition to have outdoor barbecues. The cooking at these barbecues is generally done by the man in the family.

Exercises

3: "Jingle" = a little song used in radio and TV commercials to advertise a product.
5: "Nerd" = a derogatory term used to describe someone who is considered unusual in some way. Children, who tend to identify strongly with the behavior, manner of dress, and opinions of their friends, frequently use this term to refer to someone who doesn't conform to the group.

Page 130: Communicators

- This conversation is an example of a common pattern or formula used when apologizing for a broken promise or commitment.
  1. Speaker A sets the scene by announcing that bad news is coming.
  2. Speaker A reminds Speaker B of a promise that was made earlier.
  3. Speaker A admits that the promise was not fulfilled.
  4. Speaker A gives a reason or excuse for not fulfilling the promise.
  5. Speaker A asks for forgiveness.
- The TOEFL, Test of English as a Foreign Language, is a standardized test that must be taken by most foreign students wishing to study at U.S. colleges and universities.

Chapter 8
Page 134: "It's a Shame"

- Both speakers are very disappointed and express regret throughout this conversation.
- "Out of the question" = impossible.
- In line 5, Speaker B says, "I'm afraid so." This phrase is used to express unhappy, reluctant agreement.

Page 136: "You Know What I Wish?"

- The phrase "You know what I wish?" is commonly used to initiate a topic and at the same time express a wish.
- In line 4, "I know" means "I know what you mean."

Pages 138–139: "If Only I Could Communicate with My Boss"

- In line 3, Speaker B is preparing Speaker A for an unexpected, negative response to her question when he says "Do you really want to know?"
- The expressions for admitting, "The truth is . . . " and "The fact of the matter is . . . ," are used when negative information is to follow.
- In the last line of the conversation, Speaker B makes it clear to Speaker A that he has already made up his mind to continue trying very hard when he says "Oh, don't worry."

Exercises

5: "Keep up with" = learn as quickly as.

Pages 142–143: "It's All My Fault!"

- In line 2, Speaker B is clearly angry and surprised at the news she has just heard.

Exercises

4: The Boy Scouts of America is a national organization that encourages young boys ("cub scouts" who later become "boy scouts") to be good citizens. Groups led by a scout leader, often one of the scout's fathers, take hikes in the woods, go camping, and do other activities. A Girl Scout's organization offers similar activities for young girls.

7: "Put off" = postpone.

8: "On the spot" = immediately.

Page 146: "I Regret That I Have to Fire Mr. Smith"

- In line 5, Speaker B expresses surprise at the new information when she says "Oh!"

Exercises

1: Shopping malls (large enclosed shopping centers, often situated away from the center of cities) have come to replace smaller downtown shopping areas because of the convenience they offer: large parking lots and a variety of stores in one location.

Page 148: Communicators

- In line 2, Speaker B responds to Speaker A's initiating a topic by responding "What?," meaning "What have you been thinking?"

Chapter 9

Page 152: "Nice Day Today, Isn't It"

- It is common to shorten a phrase such as "(It's a) nice day today." It is also very common to initiate a conversation with a stranger by commenting on the weather.
- Speaker B was not expecting to be spoken to and did not hear Speaker A's comment. In line 2, he responds by asking for repetition: "Pardon me?"
- In line 4, Speaker B indicates that he now understands Speaker A's comment when he says "Oh, yes."

Exercises

In all the exercises, two strangers are talking. Each exercise is an example of a common and appropriate way of initiating a conversation with a stranger.

Page 154: "Doesn't It Bother You When People Cut in Line?"

- Cutting in line and littering are annoying to most people. When Speaker A in Model 1 uses a negative question, he expects agreement. Similarly in Model 2, Speaker A expects agreement with her comment about littering.
- In both conversations, the speakers are complaining about people who are not conforming to standards of appropriate public behavior.

Exercises

4: In the United States, handicapped people by law have the right of access to public places. This includes ramps at building entrances, elevators, and reserved parking areas.

5: "Tacky" = a slang expression meaning inappropriate or not in style.

Page 156: "Let Me Put It This Way"

- In line 1, Speaker A is using technical jargon, special vocabulary that is understood by members of the profession (in this case, dentistry), but may not be understood by the general public.
- In line 3, Speaker A agrees to put what he is trying to say into simpler language so Speaker B will understand.

Page 158: "What You're Really Saying"

- In line 3, Speaker A does not want Speaker B to feel insulted. She calms him by saying "Come on, now" and advises him not to misinterpret her comment. She is insisting that nothing more was implied by her comment about his jacket.
- In line 5, Speaker B concedes that he was perhaps mistaken when he says "Oh."

Page 160: "Excuse Me for Interrupting"

- It is polite and appropriate to apologize when interrupting.

Exercises

4: There are four major TV networks in the United States: ABC, NBC, CBS, and Fox. Each has a large news department with many reporters.

5: The Internal Revenue Service (IRS) is the federal agency in charge of collecting taxes. The Central Intelligence Agency (CIA) is responsible for national security.

Page 162: "By the Way . . ."

- In line 2, Speaker B interrupts Speaker A and redirects the conversation.
- Xerox is the name of a large U.S. corporation and is also the brand name of the copying machines produced by that company. Occasionally the brand name of a very well known product will, over time, become a general label. For instance, many people refer to all copying machines as "Xerox" machines, even though they are not produced by the Xerox Company. Similarly, many refer to all cola drinks as "Coke" and to all tissues as "Kleenex," both of which are brand names.

Pages 164–165: Communicators

- By repeating the topic of Speaker A's question, "nuclear energy," in line 2, Speaker B indicates that he has a lot to say about the issue.
- In line 6, Speaker A says, "But don't you think" as a way of counteracting Speaker B's comment.
- In line 10, Speaker A interrupts Speaker B because she feels strongly about her opinion and wishes to express it.
- In line 14, "You know" is an indirect and therefore polite way of creating a pause in the discussion.
- "See eye to eye" = agree.
- "I guess not" (line 16) is a polite, indirect way of expressing agreement.

Ability/Inability

Inquiring about . . .

Can you _____?
Are you able to _____?
Do you know how to _____? **2**

Can you _____?
Is there any chance you could (possibly) _____?
Would you be able to _____? **1**

You'd consider yourself an experienced/capable _____?
You'd say you're an experienced/capable _____? **2**

Expressing Ability

I can (_____). **2**

I'm (very) good at _____ing. **2**

I've had a lot of experience _____ing.
I've had a good deal of experience _____ing.
I've had a great deal of experience _____ing.
I've had years of experience _____ing. **2**

I'm sure/I'm confident/I'm certain/I know I'd be able to learn quickly.
I'm sure/I'm confident/I'm certain/I know I could learn quickly. **2**

Expressing Inability

I can't _____.
I won't be able to _____.
I'm not going to be able to _____. **1,2**

I wasn't able to _____.
I couldn't _____. **2**

I'm not sure I can. **1**

I can't make it on _____.
I'm tied up on _____. **1**

I'd like to/love to, but I'm afraid I can't. **3**

There's nothing I can do about it.
There's no way I can get out of it.
I can't get out of it. **2**

Advice-Suggestions

Asking for . . .

What do you think (I should do)?
Do you have any advice? **6**

Any other suggestions? **4**

Do you have any suggestions/recommendations/ideas/thoughts? **4**

Can you recommend _____?
I was wondering if you could recommend _____. **4**

I need your advice on something. **4**

Offering . . .

Can I offer you { some advice?
a piece of advice?
a suggestion? } **4**

I (strongly) advise you to _____.
I urge you to _____.

I recommend that you _____.
I recommend _____ing. **4**

You should (definitely) _____.
You ought to _____.
You must _____.
Make it a point to _____.
Be sure to _____. **4**

I think you should/ought to _____.
I/I'd suggest that you _____.
I/I'd suggest _____ing.
If I were you, I'd _____.
It seems to me (that) you should _____.
Don't you think you should _____?
Don't you think it might be a good idea to _____? **4**

Maybe you ought to.
Maybe you should _____.
Maybe you should consider _____ing.
It might be a good idea to _____.
Why don't you _____? **7**

Have you considered _____ing?
Have you thought of _____ing?
Have you thought about _____ing?
Have you given any thought to _____ing?
You might consider _____ing.
How about _____ing?
What about _____ing?
Why don't you _____?
You could (always) _____.
It might be a good idea to _____.
What if you were to _____?
What if you _____ed? **4**

How about _____ing?
What about _____ing?
I suggest _____.
I'd suggest _____.
I recommend _____.
I'd recommend _____. **4**

How about _____ing?
What about _____ing?
Let's _____.
What if we _____ed?
Why don't we _____?
We could (always) _____. **4**

Take my advice!
Take it from me!
If you want my advice . . . **6**

Don't jump to conclusions!
Don't read too much into what I'm saying! **9**

Responding to . . .

Good idea!
(That's a/What a) good idea!
(That's a/What a) good suggestion.
That sounds good/great!
That sounds like a good idea! **4**

I hadn't thought of that.
That hadn't occurred to me.
That never entered my mind. **4,7**

Agreement/Disagreement

Inquiring about . . .

Wouldn't you agree (that) _____?

Wouldn't you say (that) _____?
Don't you think (that) _____? **5**

Expressing Agreement

I agree.
I agree with you.
You're right.
That's right.
That's true.
It's true.
I know. **5,8**

Absolutely!
Definitely!
No doubt about it! **5**

[less formal]
I'll say! **5**

Me, too.
I think so, too.
I feel the same way. **8**

Yes. **9**

It sure *is*. **9**

I _____ either. **9**

That's just what I was thinking.
That's exactly what I was thinking.
I couldn't agree with you more.
I feel the same way.
That's exactly what I think.
My feelings exactly.
[less formal]
You can say that again!
You took the words right out of my mouth! **5,8**

I suppose you're right.
I guess you're right.
You're probably right. **7**

I suppose you're right.
I guess you're right.
I suppose that's true.
I guess that's true.
That might be true.
That may be true.
You might be right.
You may be right.
You have a point (there).
I see your point.
I know.
Yes. **5**

Under the circumstances, I can see _____.
Given the circumstances, I can see _____.
Given the situation, I can see _____. **7**

Expressing Disagreement

I disagree.
I don't agree.
I can't agree.
I don't think so. **5**

I wish I could agree (what you), but . . .
I hate to disagree (with you), but . . .
I don't mean to disagree (with you), but . . .
I don't want to argue (with you) (about that), but . . .
I don't want to get into an argument (with you) (about that), but . . . **5**

177

I'm not so sure (about that).
I don't know (about that).
I'm not sure I agree (with you on that).
I wouldn't say that.
I wouldn't go as far as that.
I wouldn't go so far as to say that.   5

Wouldn't you agree (that) _____?
Wouldn't you say (that) _____?
Don't you think (that) _____?   5

We don't see "eye to eye" when it
    comes to _____.   9

Apologizing

I apologize.
I'm sorry.
Please forgive me.
[more formal]
Please accept my apology.   7

I apologize
Forgive me
[less formal]   } for _____ing.
Sorry   7

I'd like to apologize
I want to apologize   } for _____ing.   7
I've got to apologize

I'm sorry.
I'm really sorry.
I'm really sorry about it.
I'm very sorry.
I'm awfully sorry.
I feel terrible.
I really regret it.   3,7

I hope you'll forgive me.
Please forgive me.   7
You're going to have to forgive me.   7

Appreciation

I really appreciate it.
I appreciate it very much.   3

Approval/Disapproval

Inquiring about . . .

Do you approve of the way I _____ed?
How do you like the way I _____ed?
What do you think of the way
    I _____ed?
What do you think of how I _____ed?
Did I _____ all right?   7

Expressing Approval

Good Job!
Fine job!
Well done!
Excellent!
Very good!   7
Good idea!   7

You _____ed   { very well.
extremely well.
exceptionally well.   7
unbelievably well.

Expressing Disapproval

In all honesty, _____.
To be (perfectly) honest, _____.
To be (perfectly) frank, _____.   7

I think _____ could have been
    _____ed better.   7

You (really) shouldn't have _____ed.   7
I (really) wish you hadn't _____ed.   7
As a result of your _____ing, _____.   7

Asking for and Reporting Information

Is anything { the matter?
wrong?   4
bothering you?

What's up?   2

What makes you say that?
Why do you say that?
Why?
How come?   2,8

Perhaps you have some questions
    about _____.   2
I have a few questions.   2
I was wondering _____.   2
I've found out that _____.   2

Everybody says . . .
Everybody tells me . . .
People say . . .
They say . . .
I hear . . .   4

Asking for and Reporting Additional Information

Is there any (additional) information I
    can provide?
Do you have any (other) questions?   2

Asking for Repetition

Excuse me.   2,4,9

Pardon me?
Pardon?
What did you say?
What was that?
Come again?   4,9

Sorry. I didn't hear you.   3

What did you say?
What was that?   2

Have I had it what?!   2

Huh?
[more polite]
Excuse me?
Pardon me?
Pardon.
I beg your pardon.   4

Attracting Attention

Excuse me.   3
Charlie?   3

Certainty/Uncertainty

Inquiring about . . .

Are you certain/sure/positive?   6
Are you (absolutely) sure about that?   6
Is that definite?   6

Expressing Certainty

I'm positive/certain/sure.
I'm absolutely positive/certain/sure.
Absolutely!
Positively!   6

I know _____.
I'm sure _____.
I'm positive _____.
I'm convinced _____.   5
I definitely _____.
There's no question (in my mind), I
    _____.
I have no doubt (at all) that I _____.   6
I'm pretty certain.   6

Expressing Uncertainty

I don't know for sure.
I'm not (so) sure.
I'm not absolutely positive/
    certain/sure.
I'm not a hundred percent sure.   6

Checking and Indicating Understanding

Checking One's Own Understanding

Did you say _____?
Was that _____?   9

This Saturday evening?
7:00?
The letter to Mr. Casey?
"Tooth-Brite"?
Any minute now?   1,3,4,6

Indicating Understanding

(Now) { I understand.
I follow you.
I see.   9

Clarification

Asking for Clarification

Do you mean (to say) _____?
Are you saying _____?
Does that mean _____?   8

[less direct]
I'm afraid I'm not following you.
I'm not really sure what you're
    getting at.
I'm not quite clear as to what you
    mean (by that).
[more direct]
What do you mean (by that)?
What does that mean?
Could you clarify that for me?   9

Giving Clarification

Let me put it this way: . . .
Let me put it another way: . . .
What I'm (really) saying is, . . .
What I'm trying to say is, . . .
What I mean is, . . .
What I'm getting at is, . . .
In other words, . . .
[less formal]
Let me try that again.
Let me try that one more time.   9

What you're (really) saying is . . .
What you're trying to say is . . .
What you mean is . . .
In other words, . . .   9

I didn't say _____.   9
I just said _____.   9

Complaining

Doesn't it bother you when people
_____?
Aren't you annoyed when people
_____?
Don't you (just) hate it when people
_____?
[less formal]
Doesn't it get to you when people
_____?
Wouldn't you like to clobber people
who _____?   9
_____(ing) is (very) annoying/
inconsiderate/rude/obnoxious/
selfish/thoughtless/tacky.   9
I can't stand it when people _____.
I can't stand people _____ing.
It really bothers me when people _____.
[less formal]
I can't take it when people _____.   9

Complimenting

Expressing Compliments

I don't think I've ever seen a _____
better than _____.   7

Correcting

Giving Correction

That isn't exactly right.
That isn't quite right.
That isn't exactly correct.
That isn't quite correct.
That (really) isn't so.
I think you might be mistaken.   5
(Actually,) *the bread goes in
aisle FIVE.*   5
That just isn't so. *I DO like your
meat loaf.*   5

Responding to Correction

Thank you for calling that to my
attention.
Thank you for correcting me (on that).   5

Deduction

_____ must have _____.
_____ may have _____.
_____ probably _____.
_____ most likely _____.
I wouldn't be surprised if _____.
I bet _____.
Chances are _____.   6
_____ should have _____ed
(by now).   6
It looks like _____.
It seems as if _____.
It seems as though _____.   8

Denying/Admitting

Denying

That's not true!
That's wrong!
You're wrong!
You're mistaken!
That (just) isn't so!   5

Admitting

The truth is (that) _____.
The fact of the matter is (that) _____.   2,8

I'm afraid _____.   2
I'm afraid you're right.
I hate to admit it, but you're right.
I hate to say it, but you're right.   5
I hate to have to tell you this, but . . .
I don't feel very good about telling you
this, but . . .
I wish I didn't have to tell you this,
but . . .   7
I made a terrible mistake.
[less formal]
I (really) goofed!
I (really) blew it!   8
It's all my fault!
I'm (entirely) to blame!   8

Directing/Redirecting a Conversation

By the way, . . .
Incidentally, . . .   1,9
Before I forget, . . .
I don't mean to change the subject,
but . . .   9
Now . . .
As I was saying, . . .
To get back to what I was saying, . . .
To get back to what we were talking
about, . . .   9

Fear-Worry-Anxiety

I'm (getting) (a little)
$\left\{\begin{array}{l}\text{worried}\\\text{concerned}\\\text{anxious}\\\text{nervous}\end{array}\right\}$ about _____.   6

I'm afraid something must have
happened (to him/her/them).   6
I wouldn't be concerned.
I wouldn't worry.
Don't worry.
Don't be concerned.   6

Focusing Attention

If you ask me, . . .
In my opinion, . . .
As far as I'm concerned, . . .
I personally think . . .
As I see it, . . .
The way I see it . . .   5,9
To me, . . .
[less formal]
In my book, . . .   9
In fact, . . .
To tell the truth, . . .   6
(And) furthermore, . . .   9
I'd (just) like to point out that . . .   9
Let me say one more thing.   9
The thing to keep in mind is that . . .   9

Granting Forgiveness

That's okay.
It's okay.
That's all right.
It's all right.
Don't worry about it.
No problem.
These things happen.

We all make mistakes.
You're only human..
It's not your fault.
I understand.   7

Gratitude

Expressing . . .

Thanks.
Thanks very much.
Thank you very much.   3
Thanks/Thank you for _____.   4
Thanks a lot.   4
Thank you for *saying so.*
Thank you for *the compliment*
It's nice of you to *say that.*
It's nice of you to *say so.*   7

Responding to . . .

My pleasure.
Don't mention it.
(I'm) glad to do it.
You're welcome.   3

Hesitating

Hmm.   4,6
Uh . . .   6
Well . . .   2,4,6,7
Well, uh . . .   2
(Well,) let's see . . .   4
Well, I don't know . . .   6
You know . . .
Come to think of it . . .
You see . . .   7

Initiating Conversations

Nice day today, isn't it.   9
May I (please) speak to _____?
Can I (please) speak to _____?
I'd like to speak to _____, please.
I'd like to speak to _____, please, if
he's/she's there.
Is _____ there?   3
Hi! It's me again!   2

Initiating a Topic

You know, . . .   5,7
Let me tell you about . . .
Let me fill you in on . . .
Let me outline for you . . .
Let me advise you of . . .
Let _____ me make you aware of . . .   2
I've been meaning to ask you.   6,8
I keep forgetting to ask you.
I keep meaning to ask you.   8
(You know,) I've been thinking . . .   8
Don't you think (that) _____?
Wouldn't you say (that) _____?
Wouldn't you agree (that) _____?   5
Perhaps it's none of my business, but . . .
Perhaps I'm out of place saying so, but . . .
Perhaps it isn't my place to say so, but . . .
Perhaps I'm speaking out of turn, but . . .
[less formal]
Perhaps I'm sticking my nose where
it doesn't belong, but . . .   7
I hate to say it . . . but . . .   7

179

Regarding _____, . . .
Regarding the issue of _____, . . .
As far as _____ is concerned, . . .   9

You seem troubled/upset.
You don't seem to be yourself today.   4

Intention

Inquiring about . . .

What are you going to do (*next year*)?   6

You aren't (really) going to _____,
    are you?   6

Expressing . . .

I'm thinking of _____ing.
I'm considering _____ing.
I'm toying with the idea of _____ing.   6

Interrupting

Excuse me for interrupting, (but) . . .
Forgive me for interrupting, (but) . . .
(I'm) sorry for interrupting, (but) . . .
(I'm) sorry to interrupt, (but) . . .   9

Invitations

Extending . . .

Would you like to _____?
How would you like to _____?
Do you want to _____?
Would you be interested in _____ing?
How about _____ing?
Let's _____.   1

Would you (by any chance) be
    interested in _____ing?
You wouldn't' (by any chance) be
    interested in _____ing,
    would you?   1

We'd like to invite you (and _____)
    over for _____.
We'd like to have you (and _____)
    over for _____.
We'd like you (and _____) to be our
    guest(s) for _____.
We'd like you (and _____) to join us
    for _____.   1

Can you come?
Do you think you can come?
Do you think you'd be able to come?
Would you be able to come?
Can you make it?
Do you think you can make it?   1

Please try to come.   1

We hope you'll be able to join us.   1

If you're not busy, . . .
If you're free, . . .
If you don't have any other plans, . . .   1

Accepting . . .

I'd love to.
I'd like to.
I'd like that.
That sounds like fun.
That sounds great/terrific/wonderful.
That would be great/terrific/
    wonderful.   1

I'd be happy to/glad to.
[stronger]
I'd be delighted to/thrilled to.   1

We'd be
{
very happy
very glad
pleased
delighted
} to come.   1

We'll be looking forward to it.   1

Thanks/
Thank you for
{
asking.
inviting me.
the invitation.
}   1

I appreciate the invitation.
It's (very) nice of you to invite me.   1

Declining . . .

I'd love to, but I can't.
I'd love to, but I won't be able to.   1

Leave Taking

(You know,) I think I should
{
be going
get going
be on my way
be getting on my way
} (now).

(You know,) I (really) must be going.
I've (really) got to go now.
I've (really) got to be going now.
I (really) have to go now.
I'd (really) better go now.
I (really) need to go now.
I (really) should go now.
I have to/I've got to run.
I have to/I've got to get going.   1,9

I should get going, too.   1

Well, it's been really nice seeing
    you again.   1

I'd love to continue this
    conversation, but . . .   1

(I'm afraid) it's getting late.   9

Let's get together soon.
Let's keep in touch.
Let's stay in touch.   1

(I'll) see you soon/later/tomorrow/
    next week/ . . .   1

I'll call you.   1

Speak to you then.   1

Take care.
Take it easy.
So long.
Good-bye.
Bye.
Bye-bye.
See you.   1

Sorry I have to rush off like this.   1

(Well,) I've probably taken up enough
    of your time.
(Well,) I don't want to take up any more
    of your time.   2

I've enjoyed talking with you.
It was nice meeting you.
It was a pleasure meeting you.
I appreciate this opportunity to talk
    with you/meet with you.   2

Obligation

Inquiring about . . .

Do I have to _____?
Would I have to _____?

Would I be required to _____?
Would it be necessary (for me)
    to _____?   2

Expressing . . .

I have to _____.
I've got to _____.
I'm supposed to _____.
I need to _____.   1,3
I'm expected to _____.   1

You're supposed to _____.
You're required to _____.
You're expected to _____.
You need to _____.
You have to _____.
You've got to _____.
You must _____.
It's necessary for you to _____.
It's required that you _____.   2

We require _____ to _____.
We insist (that) _____.
We expect _____ to _____.   2

It's required/necessary/essential/
    mandatory.   2

_____ is insisting that I _____.
_____ is requiring me to _____.
[stronger]
_____ is making me _____.
_____ is forcing me to _____.   2

I don't think there's any way I can get
    out of it.   1

I'm tied up on _____.
I've got something scheduled
    for _____.   1

I didn't know that was required/
    essential/necessary/mandatory.   2

You were depending on me to _____.
You were expecting me to _____.
You had expected me to _____.   2

I don't have any obligations or
    commitments on _____.   1

We feel obligated to _____.   2

Offering to Do Something

Can I take a message?
Can I give him/her a message?
Would you like to leave a message
    (for him/her)?   3

Persuading-Insisting

Come on!
Look!
Listen!   5

Admit it!
Face it!   5

Oh, come on now.   6

Possibility/Impossibility

Inquiring about . . .

What's the possibility of _____?   6

Expressing Possibility

I might _____.
I may _____.
Perhaps I'll _____.
Maybe I'll _____.   6

Perhaps.
You might _____.

You could (possibly) _____.
There's a chance you might _____.
There's a chance you could _____.   **4**

It's a possibility.
There's a chance.
I might/may.
It could happen.
You never know!   **6**

_____ might have _____ed.
_____ may have _____ed.   **6**

Expressing Impossibility

There's no chance that _____.
There's no possibility (that) _____.
[less formal]
There's no way (that) _____.   **6**

Probability/Improbability

Inquiring about . . .

What do you think the chances are
  of _____?
What's the likelihood of _____?
What's the possibility of _____?   **6**
Is there a good chance _____?   **6**

Expressing Probability

I'll probably _____.
I'll most likely _____.
I'm pretty sure I'll _____.
Chances are I'll _____.
I guess I'll _____.
I suppose I'll _____.   **6**

In all likelihood . . .
In all probability . . .   **6**

If I had to choose between _____ and
  _____, I'd probably _____.   **6**

It should
It ought to
It'll probably
It'll most likely   } *arrive any*
In all likelihood it'll   *minute now.*
In all probability it'll
Chances are it'll   **6**

Expressing Improbability

The chances are probably not very good.
The chances are pretty slim.
That isn't very likely.
It isn't very likely.   **6**

There's not much chance of that
  happening.
I don't think that will happen.
I doubt (if) that will happen.   **6**

Promising

Offering a Promise

Promise.
I promise I'll _____.   **7**

I had promised (_____) I'd _____.   **7**

Breaking a Promise

I can't keep my promise.   **7**

I don't usually break promises.
I don't make a habit of breaking
  promises.
I'm not one to go back on my word.   **7**

Regret

It's a shame (that) _____.

It's a pity (that) _____.
I'm disappointed (that) _____.
It's disappointing (that) _____.
It's too bad (that) _____.
[less formal]
Too bad _____.   **8**

I regret (that) I _____.
I regret _____ing.   **8**

I'm sorry (that) I _____.
I'm sorry about _____ing.   **8**

I wish I hadn't _____ed.   **8**

Remembering/Forgetting

Inquiring about . . .

Remember _____?   **2**

Remember I had promised you
  I'd _____?   **7**

Indicting . . .

I remember.   **7**

I forgot.
It (completely) slipped my mind.   **2**
I forgot to _____.   **8**

Requests

Direct, Polite

Please _____.
Can you (please) _____?
Will you (please) _____?   **3**

Would you (please) _____?
I'd like you to _____.
I wish you would _____.   **3**

And while you're at it, please _____.   **3**

Could you do me a favor?
Could I ask you a favor?
Could you do a favor for me?   **3**

Would you please ask/tell _____
  to _____?   **3**

Direct, More Polite

Could you possibly _____?
Could you (please) _____?
Could I (possibly) ask you to _____?
Would you mind _____ing?
Would you be willing to _____?
Do you think you'd be able to _____?
I wonder if you could
  (possibly) _____?   **3**

Less Direct, Very Polite

I was wondering if you'd (be willing
  to) _____?
I was wondering if you could
  possibly _____?
Would you be kind enough to _____?
Would you mind if I asked you to
  _____?
Would I be troubling you (too much)
  if I asked you to _____?
Could I possibly impose on you
  to _____?
Would I be imposing on you if I asked
  you to _____?   **3**

Responding to Requests

Okay.
All right.
Sure.
Certainly.

Of course.
I'd be happy to.
I'd be glad to.
(It would be) my pleasure.   **3**

No, I wouldn't mind.
No, of course not.
No, not at all.
No problem.
It's no trouble at all.   **3**

Satisfaction/Dissatisfaction

Inquiring about . . .

How are you enjoying _____?   **8**

Expressing Dissatisfaction

I'm not enjoying _____ (at all).   **8**

Surprise-Disbelief

Quit your job?!   **6**
I didn't realize _____.   **1**

Sympathizing

That's too bad!
That's a shame!
That's a pity!
What a shame!
What a pity!
That's terrible!
That's awful!
I'm sorry to hear that.   **8**

Want-Desire

Inquiring about . . .

What do you want to do today?   **4**
I don't think I'm in the mood to _____.
I don't really feel like _____ing.   **4**

Warning

Don't _____!   **6**

(You'd better) *get out of the way!*
(You'd better) stay away from the
  _____!
(You'd better) keep clear of the _____!
You'd better not _____!
Don't _____!   **4**

If you don't (_____), _____.   **4**

Careful!
Be careful!
Look out!
Watch out!   **4**

You might _____.   **4**

You'll be disappointed.
You'll be sorry.
You'll regret it.   **6**

Wish-Hope

I wish it were cheaper   **8**

I (really) wish you hadn't _____ed.   **7**

I wish I could _____.
If only I could _____.   **8**

I hope _____.   **7**

I was hoping _____.   **8**

Page 3

Listen and choose the answer that is closest in meaning to the sentence you have heard.

1. How would you like to go to the theater tonight?
2. How about going canoeing this afternoon?
3. That sounds like a terrific idea.
4. I haven't gone to a hockey game in a long time.
5. Traveling around the world sounds great.
6. Would you be interested in buying some gold necklaces?
7. I'd be delighted to show you to your room.
8. Sunbathing on the beach sounds like a great way to spend the day.
9. How about going to a concert in the park this Sunday?

Page 7

Listen and decide what the relationship between the two speakers is.

1. A. I'm having a birthday party for the boss. Can you come?
   B. Sure. I'd love to.
2. A. We're having our daughter's wedding at the end of the summer. Do you think you can make it?
   B. I'll do my best, but I think I'll be away then.
3. A. I'm planning a surprise party for your grandfather's ninetieth birthday next Saturday. Would you be able to come?
   B. I'm not sure. Let me check my calendar and get back to you.
4. A. Phillip is putting together a barbecue at the baseball field this coming Sunday. Can you make it?
   B. I'll try as hard as I can, but I have to practice pitching Sunday.
5. A. The school government association is organizing a dance this Saturday night. Do you think you can come?
   B. I'd love to, but I'm supposed to help my mother with her dinner party Saturday.
6. A. The captain is throwing a farewell party for the crew tomorrow evening at eight o'clock. Can you come?
   B. I'm not sure. I might be on duty tomorrow. Let me check and get back to you.
7. A. We're planning to shoot that commercial for Pepsi next Tuesday. Do you think you'd be able to come?
   B. I'll try as hard as I can, but I have to meet with a client that day.
8. A. We're planning to try that new heart transplant technique in surgery this afternoon. Would you be able to come at three o'clock to observe?
   B. I'll do my best, but I have to see a patient until three o'clock.
9. A. I'm organizing a tenants' meeting tomorrow night at nine o'clock. Can you make it?
   B. Sure. That sounds like a good idea.

Page 11

Listen and choose the best conclusion.

1. A. Well, it's been nice to see you again.
   B. Yes, it has. Keep in touch.
2. A. How does eleven-thirty sound?
   B. Fine. We'll be looking forward to it.
3. A. Sally, if you're free Saturday night, would you by any chance be interested in going dancing with me?
   B. Sure, Tom. I'd love to. Thanks for the invitation.
4. A. Let's get together soon, Carol. I'm so glad we ran into each other.
   B. I know. It's been great seeing you again, Louise. I'm sorry I have to rush off, but I've got to pick up my son at school.
5. A. Well, I think I should be going now, Eddie.
   B. Me too, Larry. I have to study for an exam.
6. A. Susan, we'd like to have you and your brother over for Thanksgiving dinner. Can you come?
   B. We appreciate the invitation, but we're going to our grandparents' house for Thanksgiving.
7. A. Let's get together soon.
   B. Okay. I'll call you next time I'm in town.

Page 16

Listen and choose the answer that is closest in meaning to the sentence you have heard.

1. I'm afraid I have to get off the phone now.
2. When do you have to get back to work?
3. Let's get together soon.
4. I may be tied up until noon today.
5. I have a meeting at one o'clock, and I really can't get out of it.
6. Sorry I have to rush off like this.

Page 22

Listen and choose the best conclusion.

1. A. Rich, do you know how to drive a standard-shift car?
   B. No, I don't. I know how to drive an AUTOMATIC, but I've never driven a stick-shift before.
2. A. Jerry, do you know how to do word processing on a computer?
   B. No, I don't. I've used a COMPUTER before, but I've never used one for word processing.
3. A. So, Paula, are you an experienced legal secretary?
   B. Well, I'm a secretary, but not a LEGAL secretary.
4. A. Can you play an electric guitar, Pete?
   B. No, I can't. I've played an ACOUSTIC guitar before, but I've never played an electric one.
5. A. Do you think you could learn to operate a chain saw, Tom?
   B. Sure. I've used saws before, and I'm sure operating a CHAIN saw isn't that difficult to learn.

6. A. Do you take wedding photographs, Mr. Winston?
   B. Well, I usually do portraits, but I suppose I could take WEDDING pictures.

Page 27

Listen and choose the answer that is closest in meaning to the sentence you have heard.

1. You're going to be very disappointed with me.
2. I'm afraid I wasn't able to make a birthday cake for you.
3. I feel bad. I had promised I would help you move, but I have to study.
4. I know you were counting on me to baby-sit, but my parents won't let me.

Page 31

Listen and decide what the relationship between the two speakers is.

1. A. I'd like to give you my application for the Junior Year Abroad program.
   B. Okay, but you've got to get it signed by your academic advisor before I can process it.
   A. Okay.
2. A. I'm ready to turn in my health report for the university. Does it look okay to you?
   B. Well, before I turned in mine, I had to have it verified by my family doctor.
   A. Oh. I'm glad you told me.
3. A. Excuse me, but before I can accept this, you need to have it evaluated by our loan officer.
   B. Oh. I didn't know that was required.
   A. Yes, it's essential.
4. A. I'd like to submit my form for a marriage license, please.
   B. Okay, but you know, you're supposed to have it signed by both the bride and the groom.
   A. I know. We've done that.
5. A. Hello. Can I submit my application for the Science Foundation scholarship here?
   B. Yes, but first you must have it reviewed by your dean.
   A. Oh, I didn't know that was mandatory.
6. A. Pardon me. I'd like to report a stolen car.
   B. Okay. You're required to fill out a theft report.
   A. Oh. I didn't know that was necessary.
7. A. Excuse me. I'd like to hand in my expense report for my business trip.
   B. Okay, but it's necessary for you to have it signed by your manager before I can process it.
   A. Oh. Okay.
8. A. I'm sorry, but you need to have this note signed by your parents before I can excuse you from class.
   B. Signed by my parents?
   A. Yes, that's right.

Page 34

Listen and choose the best conclusion.

1. A. Let me tell you about some of our facilities here at Oceanside Fitness Club.
   B. All right. Thanks.
2. A. Well, Dr. Young, let me fill you in on some of the regulations here at Memorial Hospital. We require all our interns to wear green hospital clothing while on call.
   B. I understand.
3. A. Do you have any other questions about joining our church, Melissa?
   B. No, I don't. Thank you very much. I've probably taken up enough of your time.
4. A. Well, Jack, I've enjoyed talking with you about your company. Hamilton Realty sounds like quite an organization!
   B. Thank you, Dick.
5. A. Before we begin, Joel, let me advise you of some of our safety precautions for the lab. You must always wear protective glasses when working here, okay?
   B. Okay.
6. A. So, Jennifer, we'll be getting in touch with you shortly.
   B. Thank you, Mr. Leonard. I'm very grateful for this opportunity to have met you. I look forward to hearing from you.

Page 40

Listen and choose the best conclusion.

1. A. George, would you please take out the garbage before the Thompsons come for dinner?
   B. What was that, Sally?
   A. The garbage, George. I asked you to take it out before we have dinner with the Thompsons.
   B. Oh. Okay.
2. A. Adam, I'd like you to help me pick up your toys.
   B. Sorry. What did you say?
   A. I said I'd like some help picking up your toys.
   B. Oh. Sure, Mom.
3. A. Rick, can you please answer the phone? I'm in the shower!
   B. What was that?
   A. I said, please answer the phone!
   B. Okay, Frank.
4. A. Mary, will you please help me unload the dishwasher before you go out with Tom?
   B. What did you say?
   A. Would you please help me unload the dishwasher?
   B. Sure, Dad.
5. A. Larry, I'd like some help cleaning out the garage.
   B. Sorry. I didn't hear you. What was that?
   A. Can you please help me clean out the garage?
   B. Sure, Grandpa.
6. A. Betty, I wish you wouldn't open the windows while I have the air conditioning on.
   B. Excuse me? What was that?
   A. Please don't open the windows while the air conditioning is on.

B. Oh. Okay, Alan.

Page 41

Listen and decide where each conversation is taking place.

1. Linda, I wish you would be more careful when you put away the shoes after the customers have finished trying them on.
2. Mark, please dry those dishes and put them on the tables for tomorrow.
3. Tommy, please do your homework before you go to bed.
4. Will you please get me some envelopes from the stock room?
5. Certainly, Mr. Peterson. I'll run off those copies immediately.
6. I'd like you to get me another pint of blood, please.

Page 51

Listen and choose the best response.

1. Can you please carry those boxes of books for me? They're too heavy for me to lift.
2. Would you be willing to take me to my piano teacher's house?
3. Could you do me a favor, Lucy?
4. Bob, do you think you'd be able to do further research on the safety hazard problem?
5. Larry, would I be troubling you too much if I asked you to test the sound on the microphone?
6. I'd like to help you, Tina, but I'm supposed to stay here at the reception desk and greet visitors.

Page 51

Listen and choose the answer that is closest in meaning to the sentence you have heard.

1. Could I possibly ask you to help me carry those groceries?
2. I'm awfully sorry I can't help you, but I have a tennis match this afternoon.
3. Gee, I'd like to try one of your delicious fudge brownies, but I'm afraid I'm on a diet.
4. I feel terrible I can't come to your dance performance, but I'm going on a business trip that week.
5. I'd love to stay and see your slides, but I've got to cook dinner for my family.

Page 67

Listen and choose the best response.

1. Henry, you don't seem to be yourself today.
2. Mr. Ryan, can I offer you a piece of advice?
3. What's bothering you, Amy?
4. I think something's the matter with Mr. Roberts.
5. I'm so upset. My dog ran away last night!
6. Tim, don't you think it might be a good idea to relax before your presentation?

Page 73

Listen and decide where each conversation is taking place.

1. A. Watch out! That shelf is about to fall!
   B. Oh. Thanks for the warning.
2. A. Don't feed the animals! They might bite!
   B. Oh. Okay. I'm sorry.

3. A. Please keep clear of the rink. They're trying to clean the ice.
   B. Okay. Thanks for warning us.
4. A. Stay off that diving board! It's broken!
   B. Oh. Thanks for the warning.
5. A. Wendy, you'd better not disturb Mr. Pollack in 315. He's asleep.
   B. Oh. All right.
6. A. Be careful! You might fall off the roof!
   B. Thank you! I didn't see how close I was to the edge.
7. A. Don't talk so loudly! People are trying to study.
   B. I'm sorry. You're right.
8. A. Look out! He hit the ball in our direction!
   B. Oh my gosh!
9. A. Watch out! That swing is broken!
   B. Oh. Thanks. I won't use it.

Page 85

Listen and decide whether the speakers agree on a positive or negative opinion.

1. A. This restaurant is really lovely.
   B. That may be true, but don't you think that the service is slow?
   A. I guess you're right.
2. A. Those flowers are so expensive!
   B. Yes, but wouldn't you agree that they're beautiful?
   A. Yes, I suppose that's true.
3. A. There's not a lot of variety in this men's clothing department.
   B. I know, but wouldn't you say that the quality of the clothing they do have is extraordinary?
   A. Without question!
4. A. Our next space flight is going to be extremely difficult.
   B. Yes, but just think what a great contribution we'll be making to science!
   A. You're right.
5. A. That horror movie was really fantastic.
   B. But wouldn't you agree that parts of it were very dull?
   A. You have a point there.
6. A. Larry is a very creative designer.
   B. You may be right, but he's not very dependable about doing his work on time.
   A. Yes, I guess that's true.
7. A. It's been a wonderful vacation, hasn't it.
   B. Absolutely!
   A. I mean, the weather and the sights have been fantastic.
   B. I couldn't agree with you more.
8. A. The lecture on international relations was very inspirational, wasn't it?
   B. It was a little too long.
   A. You have a point there.
9. A. Our tour through the castle was fascinating, wasn't it?
   B. Without question.
   A. I mean, the architecture is amazing!
   B. I'll say!

Page 85

Listen and choose the answer that is closest in meaning to the sentence you have heard.

1. I've noticed you've been looking tired lately.
2. I hate to admit it, but I haven't been paying attention in class recently.
3. Absolutely! Joe is really improving his grades this semester.
4. It's true. The lake is much more crowded this year than it was last year.
5. I hate to say it, but it's true that I'm going bald.
6. No doubt about it! The boss has been acting strangely at work.

Page 87

Listen and choose the best conclusion.

1. A. Bob, let's go swimming later. The temperature today is supposed to go up into the seventies.
   B. Actually, Pete, I think you might be mistaken. I heard on the radio that it's supposed to be in the EIGHTIES!
2. A. I think that song was written by the Beatles in nineteen sixty-eight, wasn't it, John?
   B. No, Kathy. Actually, that's not quite right. It was written in nineteen sixty-NINE!
3. A. I see you're growing a beard, George.
   B. No, actually, Ron, that isn't so. I just forgot to shave this morning!
4. A. Bertha is celebrating her ninety-first birthday tomorrow.
   B. No, no. That's not exactly right. She's celebrating her ninety-SECOND birthday!
5. A. The safe deposit vault upstairs is open daily from nine to two.
   B. Pardon me, but that isn't so. It's open from nine to THREE.

Page 92

Listen and choose the best response.

1. Sally has great taste in clothing, don't you think?
2. Sometimes I think you can't trust anyone anymore.
3. It's cruel to be performing those experiments on healthy animals.
4. In my opinion, computers are becoming more and more important in our daily lives.

Page 97

Listen and choose the best conclusion.

1. A. Do you think our flight will be on time?
   B. Absolutely!
2. A. Do you really want to quit your job, Liz?
   B. There's no question in my mind.
3. A. Harry, are you sure you want this 35-millimeter camera and not an Instamatic?
   B. I'm positive.
4. A. Did you know the stock market was going to go up so high, or was it a lucky guess, Bob?
   B. I had no doubt it would go up.
5. A. Shirley, do you think the boss is going to give us all bonuses for Christmas?
   B. There's no way that he's going to do that!
6. A. Joe, is there enough soda in the refrigerator for our party?
   B. Oh, I'm sure there is.

Page 101

Listen and choose the answer that is closest in meaning to the sentence you have heard.

1. I'll probably get a job in a factory this summer.
2. I'm positive our candidate will win the election.
3. The doctor says she's certain Mike will be fine in a few days.
4. Alice is pretty sure she can't make it to the meeting.
5. I'm not a hundred percent sure this paint is the right color.
6. Chances are Tom will get into every medical school he applied to.

Page 101

Listen and decide where each conversation is taking place.

1. A. When will the next plane from New York arrive here in Chicago?
   B. It should be here in fifteen minutes.
2. A. How often will I receive interest for the money in my account?
   B. It'll most likely be credited to your account on the first day of each month.
3. A. How long will it take to send this clock from here to the United States?
   B. In all probability it'll take three to four weeks.
4. A. How many more minutes do you need to finish the test?
   B. It'll most likely take me another ten minutes.
5. A. How soon will we get those tickets for our trip?
   B. Chances are we'll have them in by tomorrow.
6. A. Who do you think will win the next race?
   B. It'll probably be a close one between Lucky Star and White Stallion.
7. A. What do you think we should do with all these old toys we saved from our childhood?
   B. Well, I would hate to throw them out. Let's leave them here.
8. A. When will our room be ready, sir?
   B. In all likelihood you can check in in twenty minutes.
9. A. Do you know if our food is ready? We're going to be late for the theater if it doesn't come soon.
   B. I'm sorry, ma'am. The kitchen is backed up. It ought to be ready soon.

Page 109

Listen and choose the best conclusion.

1. A. Do you think we can afford to rent this apartment?
   B. Chances are we can.
2. A. Do you think we'll have good weather for our barbecue?
   B. The chances are pretty slim.
3. A. Where will you end up on your trip to Europe?
   B. I'll most likely end up in Austria.
4. A. Do we need to buy more milk?
   B. I'm not sure.
5. A. Coach Johnson, do you really think I'm good enough to be on the squash team?
   B. Yes, Bill. Absolutely.

6. A. Can we hire someone to help with the overload of typing this week?
   B. Absolutely not!

Page 117

Listen and decide where each conversation is taking place.

1. A. Well done, Josephine! The apple pie was delicious.
   B. Thank you for saying so.
2. A. John, you did a fine job repairing my car.
   B. Thanks, Mr. Davis.
3. A. Mr. Campbell, you've been doing very good work here at the lab.
   B. Thank you. I'm so glad you approve of my work.
4. A. To tell you the truth, I don't think we've ever had such an impressive painting here in our gallery.
   B. Thank you for the compliment.
5. A. Do you really think I'm doing good work here at the front desk?
   B. Yes, you've done a fine job.
6. A. I'm so pleased with the way my hair looks.
   B. Thank you for the compliment. I hope all my customers are this pleased.

Page 122

Listen and choose the answer that is closest in meaning to the sentence you have heard.

1. Perhaps it's none of my business, but you really shouldn't talk back to the teacher.
2. Whatever prompted you to change from a Republican to a Democrat, Bill?
3. I know it isn't my place to say so, but you really could use a new suit for work.
4. I don't know what possessed you to write a letter to the president of the telephone company.
5. I guess you're right. I shouldn't have spent my last quarter on that video game!

Page 126

Listen and decide what the relationship between the two speakers is.

1. A. Mrs. Victor, I apologize for not watering the plants, but there were so many customers today that I forgot.
   B. That's okay.
2. A. Forgive me for making you stay late to type these memos, but I really need them for tomorrow.
   B. Don't worry about it.
3. A. Eddie, I'm really sorry I gave you the wrong order. Here's the cheeseburger platter.
   B. No problem.
4. A. I'm sorry I fell asleep so early last night, but I had an exam yesterday and I was exhausted. Maybe we'll have a chance to talk tonight.
   B. Okay. Don't worry about it.
5. A. I apologize for getting to your party so late, but there was a lot of traffic.
   B. That's all right.
6. A. I feel terrible about cutting your hair shorter than you wanted, but it's really very fashionable.
   B. It's fine.

184

Page 126

Listen and choose the answer that is closest in meaning to the sentence you have heard.

1. I'm sorry I never wrote you while you were in Spain.
2. Please forgive me for burning the chicken.
3. I feel terrible that you're in the hospital.
4. That's okay. I know you're not usually late.
5. Don't worry about not finishing the exam.
6. It's all right. It was only water you spilled.

Page 141

Listen and choose the best response.

1. How are you enjoying your new position at work?
2. The truth is, I'm not enjoying camp at all. I'm not very good at sports.
3. Why can't you ask your supervisor to help you iron things out?
4. I just don't feel comfortable in an administrative position.
5. So, how do you like working the night shift at the hospital?
6. Senator Smith, I'm sorry to hear your proposal wasn't passed by the Senate.

Page 149

Listen and choose the best conclusion.

1. A. You know, I wish I hadn't flunked that last test.
   B. Why?
   A. Well, if I hadn't flunked the test, I would have gotten a B in the course.
2. A. I regret that I didn't take an accounting course in college.
   B. How come?
   A. Because if I had taken an accounting course, I'd be able to handle my finances better.
3. A. You know, if I had gotten a degree in business, I would have no problem finding a job.
   B. What do you mean?
   A. Well, there are a lot of job opportunities for people with business degrees.
4. A. I wish I had gotten some brown sugar at the supermarket.
   B. Why?
   A. Then I could have made some chocolate chip cookies.
5. A. I guess Henry's plane hasn't landed yet.
   B. What makes you say that, Mary?
   A. Well, if it had landed, Henry would have called me by now.
6. A. The cake mustn't have been very good.
   B. Why do you say that?
   A. If it had been good, there wouldn't be any left.

Page 153

Listen and choose the best response.

1. Does class start at nine o'clock?
2. Has David spoken to you about fixing the radiator?
3. Those glasses are clean, right?
4. You can't do your homework without getting help?
5. Don't you think repainting the fence is a good idea?

6. She sure knows how to get the best bargains!
7. They do a great job at Scrub-Up Car Wash.
8. Do you think it's okay if I stay up late?
9. If our soccer team wins the playoffs, it will be our twelfth championship.

Page 155

Listen and choose the answer that is closest in meaning to the sentence you have heard.

1. In my book, people who don't join the union are making a big mistake.
2. Don't you just hate it when people show off on the tennis court?
3. Aren't you annoyed when someone asks for the answer to a question that you've just answered?
4. Doesn't it get to you when people leave their dirty dishes in the sink overnight?

Page 157

Listen and decide what the relationship between the two people is.

1. A. The statistics show that people with your illness have a good chance of recovering.
   B. I see.
2. A. What do you mean by you're "putting me in a place for the elderly?"
   B. Well, what I'm getting at is, we're taking you to a nursing home.
3. A. What I'm getting at, dear, is that we need a new car.
   B. Oh, I guess you're right.
4. A. I'm afraid I'm not following you. What do you mean you "gave me the grade I deserved"?
   B. Well, the fact of the matter is, you got a D on your paper.
5. A. Let me put it another way. I'm turning your apartment into a condominium.
   B. I see.
6. A. What I'm really saying is, you blew your lines.
   B. Oh. Well, I'll try to do better next time.

Page 159

Listen and choose the answer that is closest in meaning to the sentence you have heard.

1. So, what you're really saying is that you spent all the money I gave you.
2. Are you trying to say that we're sinking, Captain?
3. What you mean is that you're sick of spending so much time doing paperwork.
4. So, you're saying that you can't play that song?

Page 161

Listen and choose the best conclusion.

1. A. Sorry for interrupting, but Mr. Mason is calling.
   B. Mr. Gleason?
   A. No, Mason.
   B. Oh. Okay. I'll be right there.
2. A. Excuse me, Mr. President, but the Secretary of State is here to see you.
   B. My secretary?
   A. No, the Secretary of State.
   B. Oh. Thank you.

3. A. So, there's the tallest skyscraper in the city. It's thirty-four stories high.
   B. Wait a minute! Did you say thirty-four or FORTY-four?
   A. Thirty-four.
   B. Oh. I see.
4. A. I'm sorry to interrupt your conversation, but lunch is ready.
   B. Did you say brunch?
   A. No, lunch.
   B. Oh. That's what I thought you said.

Page 163

Listen and choose the best conclusion.

1. A. Now, regarding our new sales strategy, . . .
   B. Oh, by the way, Judy, did you know that Vicky is having a baby?
   A. Oh. No, I didn't.
2. A. Now, Roger, as I was saying, about our plans for the weekend, . . .
   B. Oh, incidentally, Jenny, we can't take my car. It's in the shop again.
   A. Oh, that's too bad.
3. A. Excuse me for interrupting, Arthur, but before I forget, I wanted to tell you the kitchen sink needs to be repaired.
   B. Oh. Okay. Now getting back to what I was saying, . . .
   A. I'm sorry, dear. I'd love to continue this conversation, but I have to run. Bye!
4. A. As far as the luncheon menu is concerned, I think we'll start with a fruit salad.
   B. I don't mean to change the subject, Liz, but where are the place cards?
   A. I don't know, Jane.
5. A. If you ask me, Peter, green looks better with that suit than blue.
   B. Oh, by the way, I just got two new tires I want to show you.
   A. Good. Let's see them.
6. A. The thing to keep in mind is to be clear and concise when you write your report.
   B. Oh, before I forget, when is it due, Professor Lawrence?
   A. It's due a week from today.

Index